Hats in Miniature

Hats in Miniature

Lyn Waring

Sterling Publishing Co., Inc.
New York

I dedicate this book to the memory of my beloved sons,
Adam Kimberly Newman, 1962–1989, and
Troy Adrian Newman, 1964–1997. All in life is God's will.

My thanks go to Clive Addison for the photography, Roy Payne for the turned wooden hat stands,
and my sister, Jan Lang, for always being there when she is needed.
I would like to thank my editor, Isabel Stein; your knowledge and patience are very much appreciated.
Thanks to Puss, my dog, my friend, and faithful companion, always there with her lovely face.
My love and appreciation, as always, to my husband, George.
Your support and encouragement make a project such as this so much easier.

Photography: Clive Addison, Claremont, Western Australia

Styling: Lyn Waring, Cottesloe, Western Australia

Diagrams and patterns: Lyn Waring, Cottesloe, Western Australia. Patterns prepared by Jeff Rosen, NYC, New York

Library of Congress Cataloging-in-Publication Data Available

10 9 8 7 6 5 4 3 2 1

Published by Sterling Publishing Company, Inc.
387 Park Avenue South, New York, N.Y. 10016
©1999 by Lyn Waring
Distributed in Canada by Sterling Publishing
℅ Canadian Manda Group, One Atlantic Avenue, Suite 105
Toronto, Ontario, Canada M6K 3E7
Distributed in Great Britain and Europe by Cassell PLC
Wellington House, 125 Strand, London WC2R 0BB, England
Distributed in Australia by Capricorn Link (Australia) Pty Ltd.
P.O. Box 6651, Baulkham Hills, Business Centre, NSW 2153, Australia
Printed in China
All rights reserved
Sterling ISBN 0-8069-4265-7

Preface

*A*s I traveled around teaching hat-making, with my earlier book, Hats Made Easy, everyone was very taken with the miniature hat samples I displayed. The miniatures enabled me show examples of how the hat designs changed by just using different fabrics and trims, so the idea of the present book was born.

People generally love hats. Making miniature hats enables them to realize their fancies without having to worry, as they would with full-size hats, about whether the hats look flattering on them.

Basic sewing skills are all you need to make these hats. The miniature hat designs given here are ideal for doll- and bear-makers. With a little imagination, you will be able to create a whole wardrobe of hats for the dolls and teddy bears of friends and family, or to use as room ornaments.

Contents

Introduction

This book concentrates on patterns for miniature hat designs. Ideas for trimming and finishing hats of any size can be found in the many and varied craft, textile, and sewing books and magazines available today. Various arrangements of flowers, ribbons, and bows give any hat design that individual look. You will see some of the many possibilities in the photos that accompany the patterns. We have also included instructions for making hat stands in medium weight cardboard for displaying your hats.

The following is a brief description of the hats you will learn how to make in this book.

Basic Hat: This is a basic design. It consists of 3 pieces: a side crown, which gives the depth of the hat; a top crown, which covers the top of the side crown; and a brim, which extends out from the side crown. Many styles can be created by extending the width of the brim or altering the height of the side crown.

Ascot: The side crown of this design is slightly shorter than, and not as straight as, the Basic Hat's side crown. The brim is the basic brim, extended in width; it can be turned up to one side.

Race Day: The side crown of Race Day is wider at the top edge than that of the Basic Hat. The brim can be turned up slightly all around the outer edge or to one side.

Easter Parade: This is a very flamboyant style. The brim turns up to one side and the side crown is shaped to enhance the brim shape.

Boater: The side crown of the Boater is shorter than that of the Basic Hat and is straight at the side. The Boater's brim is flat and is an even width all around. The brim cannot be turned up. Leaving off the brim and attaching tulle to the center back of the side crown makes the Boater a cute bridal hat.

Top Hat: This design has a high, straight side crown, with a brim that turns up slightly on the sides. We've included two side crowns for the Top Hat, so you can make it in different heights.

Chef's Hat: This design is a traditional chef's hat with a blouson top.

Cloche: This design has a very close-fitting, turned up brim. We have given two depths for the side crown pattern.

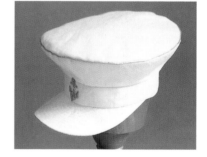

Peewee: This is a cute design. The top of the side crown shapes in with a brim that can be turned up or down. The crown can be stitched at the top edge to create an outdoors-style hat.

Basic Beret: This is a basic beret design, which can be made with or without a peak. Combining the head band and the peak gives you a cute military style cap.

3-Piece Round Crown: This design resembles an English country hat, frequently done in tweed. It has a center panel with a half circle side crown to either side of the panel. The round crown look can be altered by simply sewing a dart in the top of the center panel.

Sports Cap: The Sports Cap has a 3-piece crown and a peak. It is not suitable for combining with a brim. It can be used for a baseball cap.

5-Piece Crown: Here the crown is made from 5 sections. The 5-piece design can have a peak, like a jockey cap, or a brim.

6-Piece Beret: This is a shaped beret that can be made with or without a peak. We've given it in 2 styles. It can be a full beret or a full cap.

Trilby: This is a 4-piece crown, good for an informal hat, with a wide brim.

Country Cap: This design is similar to that worn by hunters and golfers.

Equipment & Materials

Equipment used for hat making.

This is a general equipment list. See individual projects for specifics of what is needed for each project.

✂ Sewing machine: Basic, with zigzag capability

✂ Basic straight/zigzag sewing foot, zipper foot

✂ Pintuck foot (optional)

✂ Fashion fabric and matching sewing thread for the hat. For most hats, 12 × 36 inches (30 × 92 cm) is enough

✂ Lining fabric for lining the hat

✂ Fashion fabric and fine cord for piping (optional)

✂ Fusible nonwoven iron-on interfacing (in some places sold as Vilene®), of medium weight, with fusible coating on one side.

✂ Batting (wadding): ¼ inch to ⅜ inch thick (6 mm to 1 cm)

✂ Tracing paper and paper stapler

✂ Pencil with a soft lead

✂ Pen

✂ Tape measure

✂ Clear plastic quilter's measuring ruler

✂ Pins and sewing needles

✂ Seam ripper

✂ Dressmaker's sliding rule

✂ Water-soluble marking pen

✂ Scissors of three kinds: for cutting paper, for cutting fabric, and small trimming scissors

✂ Rotary cutter and a self-healing cutting board, recommended as aids to easy, accurate cutting

ABBREVIATIONS

The following abbreviations are used in this book: CB, center back. CF, center front. CE, collar edge. BE, brim edge. R, reversed (pattern turned over).

FABRICS, LININGS, & TRIM

Various fashion fabrics were used for the hats in this book, including silk, Lurex, velvet, and linen. Any dressmaking fabric can be used to make hats. Recommended fashion fabrics

Photo 1–1. Left, pintuck foot. Center, zipper foot. Right, basic sewing foot.

are soft cottons, silks, or any natural fibers if you are a beginner. Some synthetic fabrics such as polyester are harder to work with. You don't need much fabric to make a miniature hat. A piece about 12 × 36 inches (30 × 92 cm) of fashion fabric, plus an equal amount for a lining and fusible interfacing, is enough for most of the patterns in this book. I'd recommend 16½ × 45 inches (45 × 115 cm) for the Easter Parade hat, because of the shape of the brim.

The lining should be a lightweight fabric, as is used in lining jackets or dressses, of a color that goes well with the fashion fabric. Some examples are taffeta, either silk or acetate, and lightweight cotton. Linings keep the inside of the hat neat and hide the stitching.

For trims, use your imagination; there are endless possibilities, including embroidery, ribbon embroidery, tulle, bows, and flowers. The fabrics and trims you use to make a hat can totally change its personality, as you will see in some of the group photos where several hats are made up from the same pattern. Trims make each hat you design your unique creation.

FUSIBLE IRON-ON INTERFACING

Fusible nonwoven iron-on interfacing or interlining (marketed in some countries under the name Vilene®) maintains the shape of the fabric pattern piece (see left in Photo 1–2).

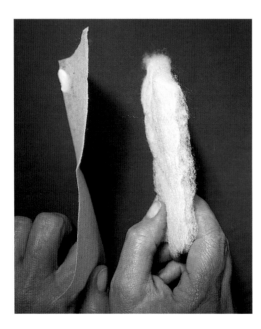

Photo 1–2. Left, medium-weight nonwoven fusible interfacing. Right, batting (wadding).

For our purposes, we need nonwoven fusible interfacing that has bonding material on one surface only. You bond it by pressing it to the fashion fabric, before you cut out the pattern pieces, as indicated in the hat instructions. If you are using a fabric with a nap, such as velvet, corduroy, or some polyesters, I recommend that you stitch the fabric to the fusible interfacing with a long machine stitch before you press the interfacing and fabric together. Each hat project indicates which pieces are to be cut from fabric + interfacing. Before you begin cutting, test that your fusible interfacing will adhere properly to your fashion fabric; modify your iron setting until it works, and get another kind of interfacing if it doesn't adhere well.

BATTING (WADDING)

Batting maintains the shape of the hat design (right in Photo 1–2). Use only polyester batting; it has a memory and always returns to its original shape. Polyester batting is the type used in quilt making. Do not use wool or cotton batting. Batting that is ¼ inch (6 mm) thick is good for the hat designs in this book. Batting comes in a variety of thicknesses and weights. You may have to split the batting you buy in order to get the correct thickness. Very thick batting can be difficult to split evenly. See the individual project instructions to find out what pattern pieces should be cut from batting.

COLLAR EDGE

The collar edge is the circumference of the head for which the hat is being designed. We will refer to this as the "total collar edge" to distinguish it from the term "collar edge," which in this book refers to the edge of the pattern piece that is part of the total collar edge. There is a collar edge on the pattern pieces for the brim, side crown, and peak.

To get the size of the total collar edge needed, measure in a circle where the hat is to be worn around the head of the bear or doll for which you are making the hat. Make sure the hair is not too squashed. Make your hat's total collar edge ¾ inch (2 cm) larger than the doll's or bear's head circumference. You may have to enlarge or reduce your pat-

terns to do this. The total collar edge for the patterns given here is 10½ inches (26.7 cm).

In traditional millinery, wooden hat blocks are used to create the shape of the crown and brim. Each shape of crown design has to match the corresponding brim block in size. The wooden crown block is usually deeper than the normal head depth. When the crown shape is cut to the required depth and then gently removed from the wooden block, a wooden collar that is the head size of the block is placed inside of the cut crown and held there with thumbtacks (drawing pins). This enables the design shape to be maintained while the crown is fitted to the corresponding-size brim block.

HAT DESIGNS

Several kinds of hat design are given in the book. The Basic Hat has a brim, a side crown (which adds height), and a top crown (across the top of the head). In some hats, the crown is pieced (piece crown). Piece crown patterns include the Sports Cap, Trilby, and 6-Piece Beret, among others. I recommend that you begin by making a Basic Hat, before you go on to other projects.

HAT SHAPE

The illustrations of the combined side crowns and brims shapes show just how different the pattern shapes are (see diagrams 2–1 and 2–2 on pages 20 and 21).

When the length of the stitch line on the top crown pattern piece is slightly smaller than the length of the stitch line on the top edge of the side crown pattern piece, the hat has a flatter look.

When the length of the stitch line on the top crown pattern is at least $\frac{3}{8}$ inch (1 cm) more than the length of the stitch line on the top edge of the side crown pattern piece, the top crown design has a more rounded look.

Generally, the patterns for brims and side crowns are interchangeable among patterns, provided the measurements of the collar edges of the pattern pieces are within $\frac{1}{16}$ inch (2 mm) of each other in length.

If you are attaching a piece crown to a brim, the total piece crown collar edge should be approximately ⅜ inch (1 cm) larger than the measurement of the total brim collar edge. If the total piece crown collar edge is the same size as the total brim collar edge, the piece crown will pull out of shape where it joins at the collar edge of the brim.

PRESSING

For laundry we iron, for hat-making we press. Ironing means that the iron is pushed back and forth. Ironing can push the fabric out of shape. For this reason, it is important to gently press when making miniature hats.

To press, as we define it here, is to let the steam from the iron penetrate the fabric (see Diagram 1–1 and 1–2). Press up and down with the iron, rather than moving it back and forth.

HINT FOR KEEPING RECORDS

When you make a hat, glue a small piece of the fabric used onto each pattern piece of that particular design. This helps you to identify a

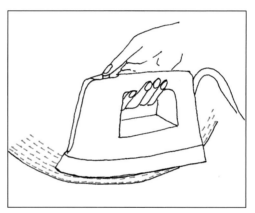

Diagrams 1–1 and 1–2. Let steam from the iron penetrate the fabric. Press up and down, rather than back and forth.

brim or a side crown that you used to create a special hat, if you want to know later on. This is especially helpful when you have substituted a pattern piece from another hat design.

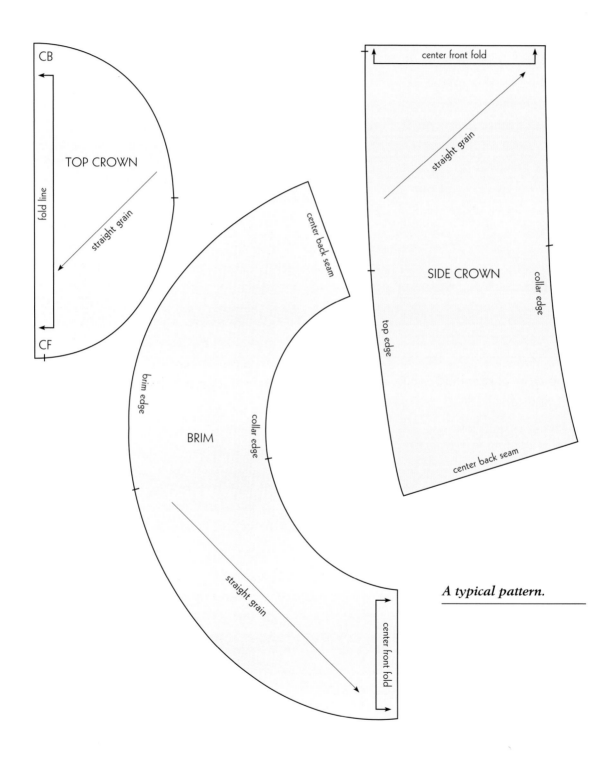

A typical pattern.

Making & Using Patterns

SUPPLIES FOR MAKING PAPER PATTERNS

You will need the following materials to make paper patterns:

✄ Tracing paper: you can use silicone-covered paper, used for baking

✄ Ruler: the clear plastic kind used for patchwork is ideal

✄ Pencil: soft lead pencil with a fine point for tracing

✄ Pen: for writing details on pattern

✄ Scissors for cutting paper

✄ Stapler

✄ Dressmaker's sliding measure

✄ Dressmaker's pins

MEASUREMENT

We suggest that you make the Basic Hat first. At some point, you may need to know the total collar edge of hat pieces to enlarge or reduce them, or to mix pieces with another pattern. Diagrams 2–1 and 2–2 (on pages 20 and 21) compare the brim and side crown pattern shapes of various hats, so you can get an idea of their variety.

The measurement of the patterns for collar edge of the brim and the measurement of the collar edge of the side crown need to correspond. To measure the collar edge of the brim, with the tape measure upright on the collar edge seam, measure from the center back seam stitch line to the center front fold line. To find out the length of a side crown piece, with the tape measure upright and on the collar edge stitching line, measure the side crown collar edge from the center back seam line to

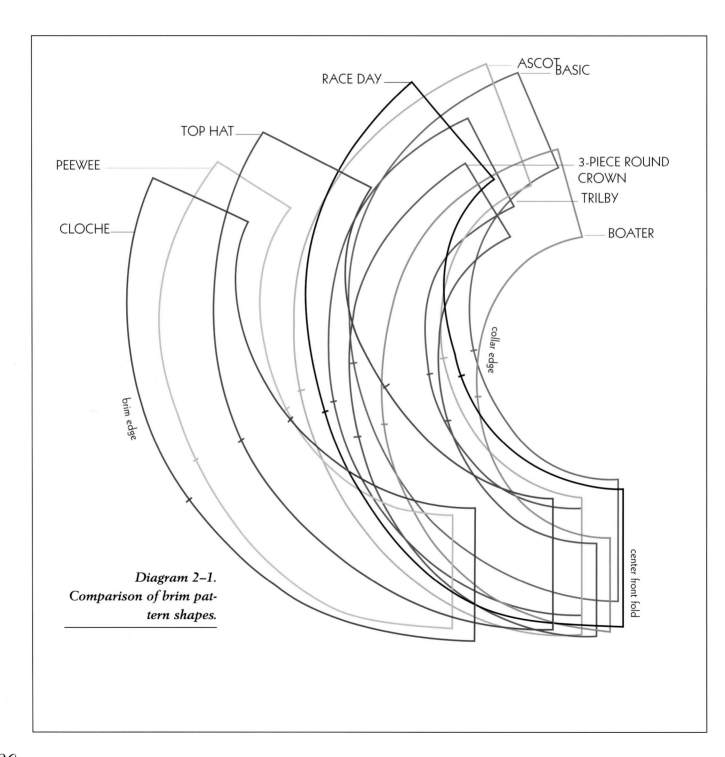

RACE DAY

ASCOT

BASIC

TOP HAT

PEEWEE

3-PIECE ROUND
CROWN

TRILBY

CLOCHE

BOATER

brim edge

collar edge

center front fold

Diagram 2–1.
Comparison of brim pat-
tern shapes.

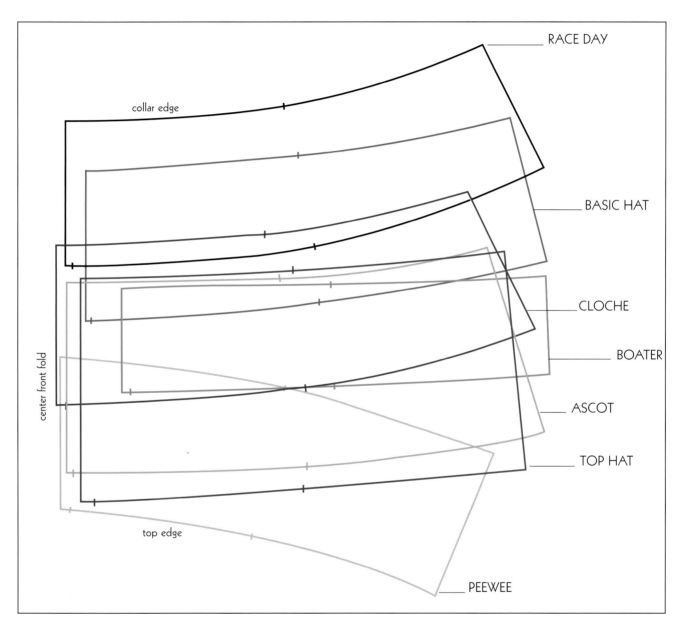

RACE DAY

collar edge

BASIC HAT

CLOCHE

BOATER

center front fold

ASCOT

TOP HAT

top edge

PEEWEE

Diagram 2–2. Comparison of side crown pattern shapes.

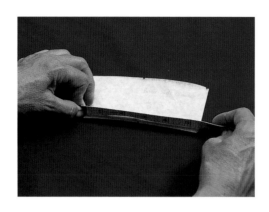

Photo 2–1. Measuring the collar edge of a pattern piece.

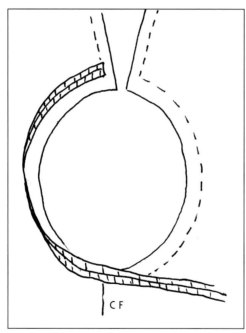

Diagram 2–3. Measuring the collar edge of the brim.

C F

the center front fold line. Photo 2–1 shows measuring the collar edge of the side crown with a tape measure. Measure the brim collar edge from the center back seam line to the center front fold line (Diagram 2–3) to ascertain the brim length.

CREATING A PAPER PATTERN

1. Adjusting size. Pattern pieces are given at 100% of size, without seam allowances, unless noted otherwise. The total collar size of each pattern is 10½ inches as given (26.7 cm). After you measure your doll's or bear's head circumference, you may want to enlarge or reduce the pattern to fit. Measure your doll's head around the circumference of the head or at the position you want the hat to be worn. Make sure the hair is not too squashed down. **Note:** the total collar edge of the paper pattern should be at least ¾ inch (2 cm) larger than the circumference of the head it will sit on. When the hat is stitched together, the bulk of the collar edge will make the hat size smaller by about ½ inch (1 cm) if you

use a lightweight cotton fabric, or more for a heavy fabric. You may need to enlarge or reduce your pattern. For example, if the animal's head circumference is 13 inches, you want to enlarge the pattern pieces so they will have a total circumference of 13½ inches. Since they are 10½ inches (26.7 cm) circumference in the book, you need to enlarge the pattern pieces at 130% (13.5 inches divided by 10.5 inches). You can easily do this on a photocopier. Add seam allowances after increasing or reducing the pattern.

2. Tracing half patterns. Many of the pattern pieces in the book are given as half patterns. You can tell they are half patterns because they have a foldline. To trace a pattern piece, get a piece of tracing paper at least twice the size of the pattern piece to be traced. Measure and mark a line midway down the tracing paper.

3. Place the tracing paper over the pattern, aligning the drawn line with the pattern's fold line. Holding the paper steady with one hand, trace over the pattern shape (Photo 2–2).

Photo 2–2. Tracing a pattern piece with fold line on paper's fold.

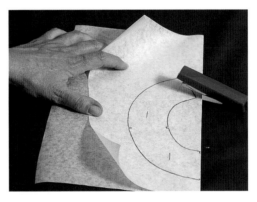

Photo 2–3. Staple the folded tracing paper before cutting, to hold both layers.

4. Fold the tracing in half along the drawn fold line, and staple the folded pattern paper halves together (Photo 2–3). Staples hold the paper steady, making cutting the pattern outline easier. Before you cut out the paper pattern piece, draw on the seam allowances as follows: Add ⅜ inch (1 cm) to the center back seam. Add ¼ inch (6 mm) to all other seam allowances except peak or brim outer edges, which should be

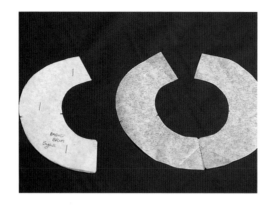

Photo 2–4. Left, the folded paper pattern, with seam allowances added. Right, the unfolded paper pattern.

Photo 2–5. Clip notches in paper pattern.

$\frac{1}{16}$ inch or 3 mm. (Don't add any seam allowances on the fold lines, of course.) Extend the tick marks on the pattern pieces so they cross the seam allowance as well.

5. Cut out the pattern shape through both thicknesses of paper if it is a folded pattern piece. Follow the pattern shape carefully and be sure there are no extra dents in the curve at the fold line after the pattern is cut out. This will give a nice rounded shape at the center front pattern edge (Photo 2–4).

6. Where each tick mark crosses the outline of the seam allowance, clip a notch by cutting a small V into the seam allowance of the pattern (Photo 2–5). These are alignment notches to help you match up the pattern pieces when sewing time arrives, so be sure to transfer them accurately.

7. Write design details and the size on each pattern piece for future reference. Note on each piece how many to cut from fashion fabric + fusible interfacing, lining, and batting, and the pattern's size.

8. Remove the staples from the folded paper pattern pieces and open them out. Check that the shapes at the center fronts have nice, rounded edges (Photo 2–6).

The exception to the general pattern preparation instructions above is the Easter Parade hat, which is asymmetrical. See that project for specific pattern copying and assembly instructions.

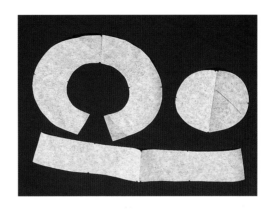

Photo 2–6. A top crown, side crown and brim paper pattern.

CUTTING FABRIC

After you have your paper patterns, you are ready to place them on fabric. Check the pattern instructions and see which pieces need to be cut from fabric + fusible interfacing. Press a piece of interfacing to the back of the fashion fabric that is large enough to fit the pattern pieces, as described earlier in Fusible Iron-on Interfacing. Patterns are always used as the complete shape and are placed flat on the fabric + interfacing surface.

Each pattern piece has a grain line marked. The grain line is simply a guide for the placement of the pattern on fabric. Align the grain line arrow with straight grain of the fabric and pin the pattern piece to the fabric.

Cutting is very important for paper patterns and the fabric + interfacing as well. This is explained in detail in the Basic Hat chapter. Take a little extra time to carefully cut the fabric + interfacing and batting (wadding) pattern pieces. It makes sewing the hat together much easier.

NOTCHES

It is important to mark notches with a water-soluble pen and clip them before you remove the pattern piece from the fabric. The notch should be $1/32$ inch (2 mm) in depth. The notches make the joining of pattern pieces much easier. You will quickly find out their importance if you don't mark them. For lamé or metallic type fabric, use a spot of white typing correction fluid to mark the notches.

STITCH LENGTHS

The rule of thumb for your stitch length is that it should be short enough to hold the garment together and long enough for easy unpicking. Mistakes are made! You want to be able to easily rip out a seam if necessary. Normal stitch length (NSL) is 10 to 11 stitches to an inch (2.5 cm). Long stitch length (LSL) is 6 to 7 stitches per inch (2.5 cm).

STITCHING SEAMS

All construction is done with right sides of fabric facing each other, unless noted otherwise. Where possible when sewing a hat, avoid bulky seams. The following is a method of sewing a secure seam without tying knots:

a. Start stitching the seam by placing the machine needle in the work ⅜ inch (1 cm) in from the edge; then reverse-stitch back to the edge.

b. Stitch forward from the edge, over the previous few stitches to the other end of the seam.

c. Reverse-stitch back ⅜ inch (1 cm) into the previous few stitches.

d. Trim the thread ends back to about 1/16 inch (2 mm) from the seam.

e. Peel the interfacing away from the seam allowance, and trim it back to the seam stitching.

f. Clip the corners of the seam allowances at an angle.

g. Finger-press the seam allowances open.

Piping

Piping is made of strips of fabric cut on the bias, wrapped around thin cord. It can be the same color as the hat or a contrasting color.

MATERIALS FOR PIPING

✂ Fabric

✂ Fine cord for piping (medium thickness knitting cotton is ideal)

✂ Rotary cutter and self-healing cutting board

✂ Pins

✂ Dressmaker's slide rule

✂ Clear plastic patchwork ruler (recommended) or a steel edge ruler

It is necessary to consider the thickness of cord to be inserted and the width of the seam allowances. In miniature hats the cord for the piping is fine, No. 5 knitting cotton.

MAKING PIPING

1. Cut a bias strip of fabric 1 inch (2.5 cm) wide by the length that is required (photos 3–1and 3–1a). You can piece bias strips together, if necessary, to get the length you need.

2. A zipper foot (Photo 3–2, Diagram 3–1) is generally used to encase the cord in the bias strip of fabric. Optional: A pintuck foot, combined with moving the needle position left or right, is ideal for making piping (Photo 3–3). If your machine does not have a

Photo 3–1. Cutting bias strips, using a rotary cutter quilter's ruler, and self-healing cutting mat.

Photo 3–1a. Overhead view of same procedure.

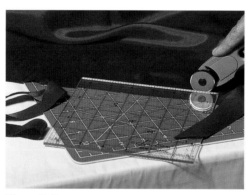

Photo 3–1

Photo 3–1a

Photo 3–2. Using a zipper foot to make piping.

Photo 3–2

Diagram 3–1. Using a zipper foot to make piping.

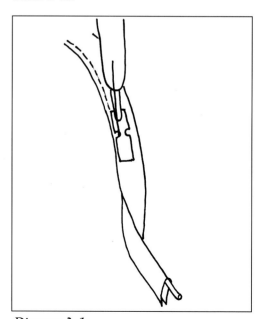

Diagram 3–1

Photo 3–3

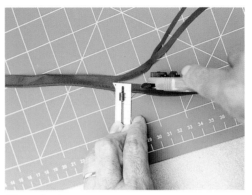

Photo 3–4

Photo 3–3. Using a pin-tuck foot to make piping.

Photo 3–4. Measuring and trimming the seam allowance of the piping.

pintuck foot, find one that has a groove in the base of the foot. This enables the cord to be held snugly in the fabric as you sew.

3. Using a long machine stitch, encase the cord in the bias strip.

4. Trim away the excess seam allowance, using a dressmaker's slide rule to measure the seam allowance and a rotary cutter (Photo 3–4, Diagram 3–2), so the seam allowance is ¼ inch (6 mm).

5. We now have a length of piping with exactly the right seam allowance for our miniature hat project.

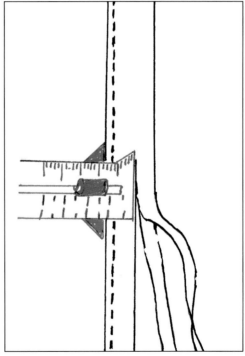

Diagram 3–2

Diagram 3–2. Measuring the seam allowance with a dress-maker's slide rule.

ATTACHING PIPING: GENERAL NOTES

To highlight the stitch line so it will be easily noticed when you sew the side crown to the top crown, change the color of the bobbin thread to something other than the color used in sewing the hat. For white or light-colored hats, use a pale pastel colored thread to highlight the stitch line. This thread is not removed later.

We will use the side crown pattern for as an example. The same idea applies to all piping in our hat projects.

1. Change the color of the bobbin thread to a contrasting color.
2. To attach piping, use the same machine foot used to make the piping. Turn the side crown piece with the right side in.
3. Starting at the center back seam at the top edge of the side crown, place the piping on the fabric, with raw edges of piping and fabric aligned. Leave approximately a 1 inch (2.5 cm) tail of piping extra before attaching. Pin or baste it in place if you want. Lower the needle into the stitching line of the piping (see Photo 3–5).
4. Using the stitching on the piping as a guide, stitch the piping to the fabric of the side crown. Be sure to keep the edge of the piping aligned with the edge of the side crown. Continue stitching until about 2 inches (5 cm) from the beginning (see Diagram 3–3 or Photo 3–6).
5. Fold a miter pleat in the beginning tail of the piping (see Diagram 3–4 and Photo 3–6 for detail of miter). To make this easier, pull the top machine thread through to the back and pull both threads straight to the right. Fold the tail of piping to the right and toward you. This will create a miter pleat in the seam allowance of the piping. Pin the miter in place.

Photo 3–5

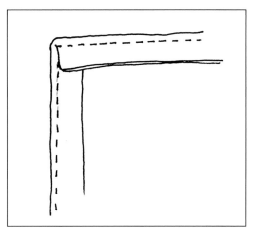

Diagram 3–4

Photo 3–6

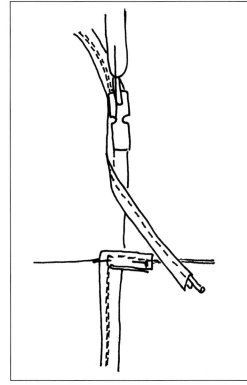

Diagram 3–3

Photo 3–5. Applying piping to a side crown edge.

Diagram 3–4. Folding a miter pleat in the piping tail.

Photo 3–6. Stitch up to 2 inches (5 cm) from where you started stitching. First piping tail pinned in a miter pleat.

Diagram 3–3. Stitch until 2 inches (5 cm) from beginning.

Photo 3–7. Lay the loose piping over the folded first end of the piping.

Photo 3–8. Make just 1 stitch into the tail of piping beneath.

Photo 3–7

Photo 3–8

Diagram 3–5. Piping over the folded tail.

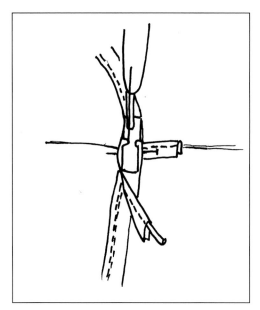

Diagram 3–6. Pull the top piping to the right.

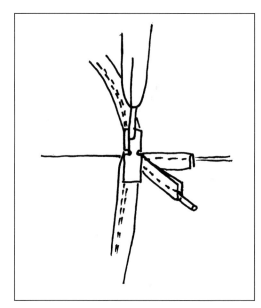

Diagram 3–5

Diagram 3–6

6. Lay the loose part of the piping that is to be attached over this folded tail, keeping the raw edges on top and in line with each other (Photo 3–7, Diagram 3–5).

7. Continue stitching until the needle is just catching the edge of the miter, just one stitch into the tail beneath. Leave the machine needle down (Photo 3–8). Raise the machine foot.

8. Pull the top piping end to the right, lower the machine foot, and continue stitching along the piping seam for about ⅝ inch (1.5 cm); see Diagram 3–6 and Photos 3–9 and 3–10.

9. Cut the second end of the piping back to a length of 1 inch (2.5 cm), creating a second tail.

When you roll the seam allowance of the piping back to the batting side, there should be a fine line of piping showing (Photo 3–11).

Photo 3–9. Pull the top piping to the right.

Photo 3–10. Continue stitching for about ⅝ inch (2 cm).

Photo 3–11. A fine line of piping shows over edge of side crown.

Hat Patterns & Instructions

Basic Hat

This is a basic design. Many styles can be created by extending the width of the brim or altering the height of the side crown. The directions for the Basic Hat also apply to Ascot, Race Day, Top Hat, Easter Parade, and Cloche.

Hats made with the Basic Hat pattern. Center, black polka dotted fabric with daisy trim, made with a full side crown. Right, white linen hat with red ribbon and cherry trim, made with a shortened side crown. Left, white polka dotted fabric with black bow trim, made with a full side crown.

Materials

✄ Fashion fabric

✄ Fusible nonwoven iron-on interfacing

✄ Batting (wadding)

✄ Lightweight lining fabric such as taffeta

✄ Decorative cord for the lining (optional)

✄ Fine cord for piping*

✄ Contrasting color fabric for making piping*

✄ Materials for pattern making (see Pattern chapter)

Piping is optional.

Pieces to Cut*

Fashion fabric + interfacing: 1 side crown, 1 top crown, and 2 brims (1R)

Lining: 1 side crown and 1 top crown

Batting (wadding): 1 brim, 1 side crown, and 1 top crown

*Patterns on page 54.

Directions for Starting

1. Press fashion fabric to the interfacing so the interfacing bonds to the wrong side of the fabric (Photo 1). See the Interfacing section for details. For hard-to-adhere fabrics, stitch the interfacing to the fabric before pressing.

2. To cut the brim, you will cut through two thicknesses of fabric to make two brim shapes, so fold the fabric + interfacing over to a size to fit the brim pattern, with interfacing side facing out (Photo 2). Place the brim pattern on the interfacing side of the fabric + interfacing. Pin at center front, in the middle of the pattern, and then at each of the center back seams. Too many pins distort the

Photo 1. Put the side of the interfacing with the bonding material facing the wrong side of the fabric. Press the fashion fabric to fusible interfacing.

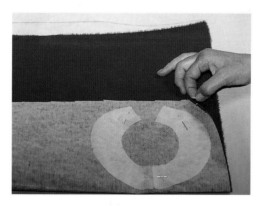

Photo 2. Pin the pattern pieces that require interfacing to the fabric + fusible interfacing with the interfacing side up.

pattern shape. Take care when cutting out your fabric. Precise cutting makes sewing patterns together much easier. A rotary blade and a cutting mat make precise cutting easier (Photo 3).

3. Before you remove the pattern pieces from the fabric, clip and mark the notches with a water-soluble pen (Photo 4).

4. To cut the side crown and top crown: With the interfacing side facing you, pin the side crown and

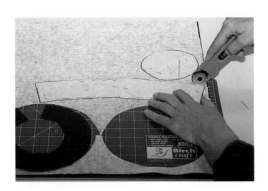

Photo 3. Cutting out side crown and top crown with a rotary cutter.

Photo 4. Clip the notches before removing paper pattern from the fabric.

Photo 5. The fabric + interfacing piece, with stitching around the edges.

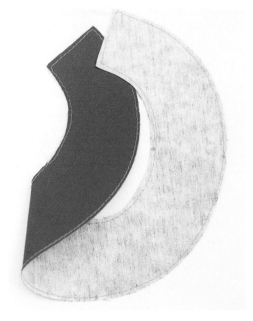

top crown pattern pieces in place on the fabric + interfacing. The top crown is always placed on the fabric's bias. Then cut. If the fabric and interfacing aren't adhering after you cut pattern pieces, press each pattern piece on the fabric side, making sure that the fabric and interfacing notches are in line with each other. Then stitch around the pieces just inside the cut edge, using your longest machine stitch (Photo 5).

5. Cutting batting: After cutting out batting pattern pieces, clip and mark the notches with a water-soluble pen. Split the batting pieces to get the correct thickness of batting, if necessary (Photo 6).

6. Cut out the lining pieces, 1 side crown and 1 top crown.

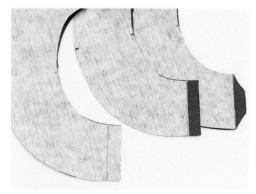

Photo 6. Carefully split the batting into layers.

Photo 7. Left: Fabric + interfacing seam of the brim, showing the seam allowance. Center: The fusible interfacing here was trimmed back to the stitch line. Right: The seam allowances are clipped at an angle at the points.

Photo 7

Photo 8

Photo 8. Trimming back the fusible interfacing to the stitch line.

Photo 6

Order of Sewing

1. Sew up the center back seam of each fabric + interfacing brim piece (left in Photo 7), and sew up the center back seam of the side crown fabric + interfacing.

2. Peel the interfacing away from the center back seam allowances, and trim the interfacing back to the stitching line (Photo 8; center in Photo 7). Clip the corners of the seam allowances (Photo 9).

Photo 9

Photo 9. Clipping off the points of the seam allowances at an angle.

Photo 10. Finger pressing the seam allowances flat.

Diagram 1. Seam allowance pressed open and ends trimmed off.

Photo 10

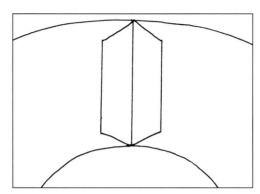

Diagram 1

Photo 11. How the finished seam allowance looks.

Photo 12. Measuring and clipping the ½ inch (1 cm) center back seam on the batting (wadding).

Photo 11

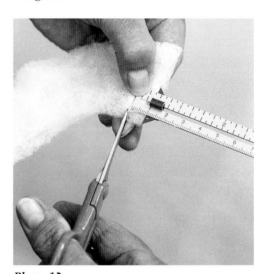

Photo 12

Diagram 2. Measure and clip notches in each end of seam allowances of the batting.

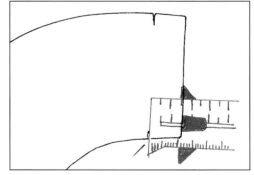

Diagram 2

3. Finger-press the seam allowances flat (Photo 10; Diagram 1).

Photo 11 shows how the center back seam allowances should look after stitching, trimming off interfacing, clipping seam allowance corners, and finger pressing.

Stitching Batting

1. Fold the batting pattern pieces of the brim and side crown in half at the center front notches. Clip a notch ⅜ inch (1 cm) in from the center back seam of the brim and do the same at the center back seam of the side crown (Photo 12, Diagram 2).

2. Overlap the center back seam allowances of the batting brim at the notch marks and pin the center back seam (see Diagram 3).

3. Stitch down the center back seam line of the batting brim from clip to clip, turn, move out into the seam allowance from this row of stitching by ¹⁄₁₆ inch (2 mm), and stitch back to beginning (see Diagram 4).

4. After stitching, trim the excess batting seam allowance back to the stitching line (Photo 13).

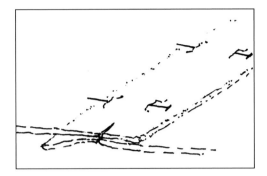

Diagram 3. Overlap and pin in place the center back seams of batting.

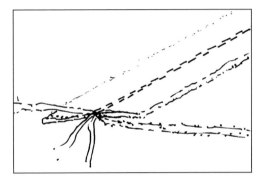

Diagram 4. Two rows of stitching at batting center back seam line.

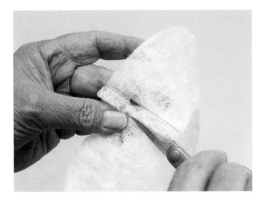

Photo 13. Trimming the excess batting of the seam allowances back to the stitch line after the ends are sewn together.

Photo 14. The batting brim stitched to the fabric + interfacing brim. Photo 14a. Closeup.

5. Sew up the batting side crown center back seam in the same way, and reduce its bulk by trimming also.

Sewing the Brim

1. Pin the batting brim to the wrong side of a fabric + interfacing brim piece, aligning them at their notch marks. Pin them together first at the center back, then at the center front, then at each side.

2. Using a long machine stitch, sew the batting brim to the fabric + interfacing brim at the inside collar edge, and then at the outside brim edge. Photos 14 and 14a show them sewn together.

3. Take the second fabric + interfacing brim piece and the fabric + interfacing + batting piece you made in step 2. Pin the brim pieces together, with right sides of fabric facing; pin first at the center back, then at the center front, then at each side.

4. Stitch the pieces together at the brim (outer) edge, starting approximately ⅜ inch (1 cm) before the center back seam (Diagram 5), continuing around, and stitching ⅜ inch (1 cm) over

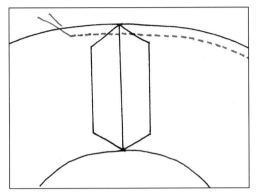

Diagram 5

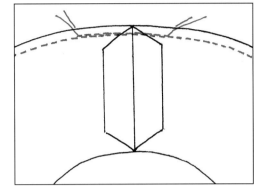

Diagram 5a

Diagram 5. Stitching the brim pieces together. Diagram 5a. Overstitching the start.

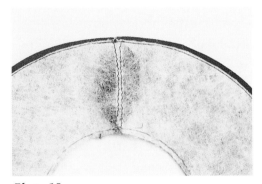

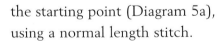

Photo 15

Photo 15a

Photo 15. The batting and fusible interfacing trimmed back to the stitch line. Photo 15a. Closeup.

the starting point (Diagram 5a), using a normal length stitch.

5. Unpick the long machine stitches holding the batting to the brim on the brim's outer edge.

6. Trim the batting back to the stitching on the outer edge of the brim (Photos 15 and 15a; Diagram 6).

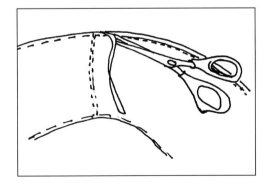

Diagram 6. Trim the batting back to the stitching.

Photo 16. The brim stitched together at the collar edge.

Photo 17. Hold the steam iron over the brim.

Photo 18. Finger-press the brim edge.

7. Turn the brim right side out.

8. Using a long machine stitch, stitch the brim layers together, ¼ inch (6 mm) in from the collar edge, aligning the notches at collar edges of the brim. Photo 16 shows the brim stitched at the collar edge.

9. Hold a steam iron over the brim (do not press), allowing the steam to penetrate at the brim edge to soften the fabric (Photo 17).

10. Finger-press the brim, rolling the seams so they sit evenly on each other (Photo 18). Finger pressing makes stitching the brim easier.

Stitching the Lines in the Brim

You can use a contrasting color of thread, as shown here, or the same color of thread as the fabric to top-stitch the decorative lines in the brim.

1. For the first line, it is important to stitch as close to the brim edge as possible, to compact the seams. Place the machine needle 1 inch (2.5 cm) before the center back seam, on the outer edge of the

brim, and start stitching (Diagram 7). Continue around the outer edge of the brim until you are back to where the stitching began (Diagram 8).

2. Don't lift up your needle, but proceed snailwise in a spiral, moving gradually away from the first line of stitching. Continue stitching until there is a space of about ⅛ inch (or about 4 mm) between the first row of stitching and the second circle.

3. Keep your ⅛ inch space between circles and continue stitching around the brim in a spiral, spacing each line of stitching about ⅛ inch (4 mm) from the previous row of stitching.

Note: With most of the brim shapes, you will arrive at the center back collar edge stitch line of the brim, and have an unstitched space toward the front of the brim (Photo 19, Diagram 9). This space will vary with each brim design (Photo 20). Add a line of stitching in the space until the brim shape is completely stitched to the collar edge (Photo 21).

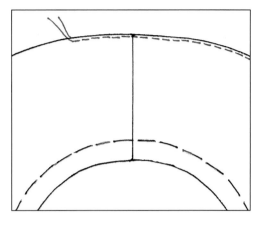

Diagram 7. Starting to topstitch the brim.

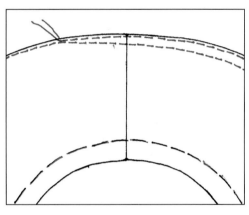

Diagram 8. Keep stitching to where you started.

Photo 19. The stitching at the center back collar edge of the brim.

Diagram 9. The spiral stitching around the brim.

Photo 19

Diagram 9

Photo 20. The space at the center front of the collar edge of the brim

Photo 21. The completed stitching at the center front of the collar edge.

Photo 20

Photo 21

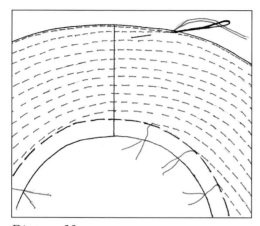

Diagram 10

Photo 22

Photo 24

Photo 23

Diagram 10. Ending off the thread between the rows.

Photo 22. End off the brim threads in between the spaces.

Photo 23. Trimming the threads on the brim.

Photo 24. Pressing the stitched brim.

4. Hide the loose ends of the threads from the start of the stitching at the outer brim by pulling both the top and bobbin thread to one side of the fabric and threading them through a big-eyed hand sewing needle. Stitch it in between the line spaces (Diagram 10 and Photo 22) and clip off the excess tail (Photo 23).

5. Hold the iron above the stitched brim and let the steam penetrate. Press the brim firmly (Photo 24).

Photo 25. The batting pinned inside the side crown.

Photo 26 and 26a. The fabric + interfacing and the batting side crowns stitched together at top and collar edges, and closeup of same.

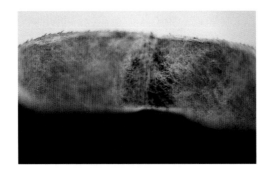

Stitching the Batting to the Side Crown and Top Crown

See the piping chapter if the side crown is to be piped.

1. With the right side of the fabric + interfacing side crown out, place the batting side crown inside the fabric side crown. Align the batting to the fabric + interfacing unit and pin, first at the center back, then the center front, then at each side (Photo 25).

2. With a long machine stitch, stitch the batting side crown and fabric side crown together a little bit in from the inside collar edge, and then at the top edge. Photo 26 and 26a show the stitched unit.

3. Stitch the batting top crown to the fabric + interfacing top crown on the wrong side of the fabric.

Sewing the Top Crown to the Side Crown

1. Turn the side crown inside out, batting facing you. Place the top crown inside, so right sides of fabric are facing each other. Align notches and pin, first at the center back, then at the center front, then at each side.

2. Stitch the side crown to the top crown with the side crown facing upwards; start stitching ⅜ inch (1 cm) before the center back seam (Photo 27).

3. As you stitch, slightly pull the edge of side crown, keeping this edge in line with the curve of the top crown.

4. Continue sewing around the top of the side crown and stitch ⅜ inch (1 cm) over where stitching began (Photo 28 shows the stitched unit).

5. Unpick the long stitching that holds the batting to the side crown and top crown pieces. Trim the batting back to the stitching line that holds the pieces together (Photo 29).

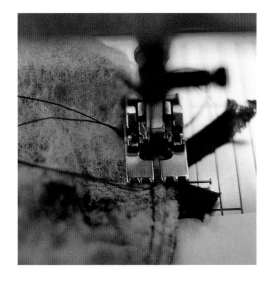

Photo 27. Stitching the side crown to the top crown at the edge.

Photo 28. The top crown stitched to the side crown, both still wrong-side out.

Photo 29. The same unit with the batting and fusible interfacing trimmed back to the stitching line.

Photo 30. Filling the inside of the side crown with steam.

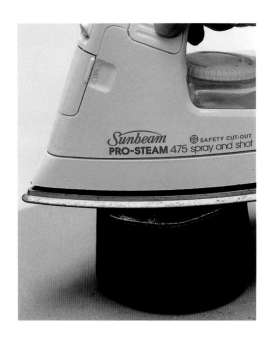

6. Turn the crown unit right-side out.
7. Place the crown unit top down on an ironing surface; then hold the steam iron over the inside of the side crown, allowing the steam to fill the inside (Photo 30).
8. Put a hand inside the side crown and, with the other hand, finger-press around the seam edge of the side crown to the top crown (Photo 31).

Joining the Crown Unit to the Brim

1. Rest the collar edge of the brim over the collar edge of the side crown, with right sides facing; align notches. Pin them together, first at the center back, then at the center front, then at each side.

Photo 31. Finger-press the top of the side crown.

2. Working from inside the side crown, stitch the crown and brim together, starting ⅜ inch (1 cm) before the center back seam; keep a ¼ inch (6 mm) seam allowance in from the collar edge (Photo 32).

Photo 32. Stitch the brim and side crown together on the collar edge.

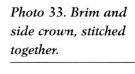

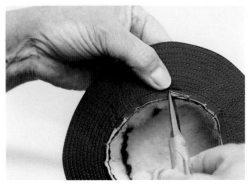

Photo 34

Photo 33

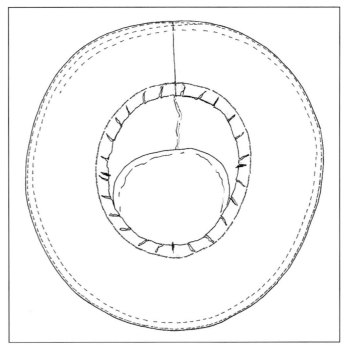

Diagram 11

Photo 33. Brim and side crown, stitched together.

Photo 34. Clipping into the collar edge seam allowances.

Diagram 11. Clip the seam allowance to within ¹/₁₆ inch (2 mm) of the seam line.

3. Continue sewing around the side crown and overstitch ⅜ inch (1 cm) from where stitching began. Photo 33 shows the brim stitched to the crown.

4. Clip around the collar edge of the brim seam allowance only, to within ¹/₁₆ inch (2 mm) of the stitch line. Leave approximately ⅜ inch (1 cm) between each clip (Photo 34, Diagram 11).

Photo 35 shows the hat, ready to be lined.

Lining

Photo 35. The hat, nearly finished.

The lining covers all the seams and threads inside the hat and gives it a tidy finish. The brim is not lined.

1. Sew up the center back side crown lining seam and stitch together the top and side crown lining sections, matching notches, with right sides of fabric facing.

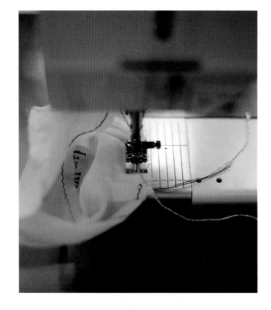

Photo 36. Tacking metallic thread onto the lining with zigzag stitches. Tacking stitches are done in red here so you can see them.

2. To stitch decorative cord to the lining, as seen in Photo 36, use a small zigzag stitch and a cording foot or similar foot. Use invisible thread or thread the same color as the fabric. This is done before the lining is stitched into the hat. On the right side of the lining, starting at the center back seam, stitch a decorative cord or a fine ribbon ¼ inch (6 mm) in from the collar edge of the lining, leaving a 4 inch (10 cm) length of cord before you start and after you stop (Photo 37, right). Pull the stitching thread ends through to the wrong side of the lining fabric and tie them off.

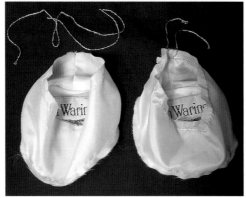

Photo 37. The lining. Left, metallic cord not yet sewn in. Right, assembled, with personalized name tag sewn on.

52

3. Finger-press the lining collar edge seam allowance to the wrong side of the lining side crown. Pin the lining into the inside of the fabric side crown on the stitch line of the brim, with wrong sides of fabric facing. Align the notches and pin first at the center back, then at the center front, then at each side.

4. Hand-stitch the lining to the inside of the side crown, easing the decorative cord or ribbon to cover the stitch line joining the side crown to the brim (Diagram 12).

Tie a bow in the cord (Diagram 13). The hat is finished.

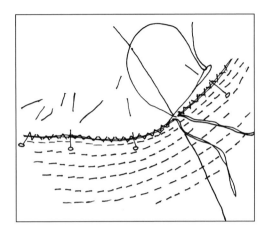

Diagram 12. Hand-stitch the lining to the side crown.

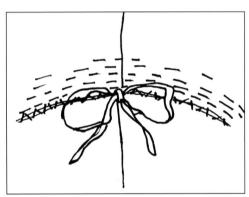

Diagram 13. Tie a bow in the decorative cord to finish.

Basic Hat

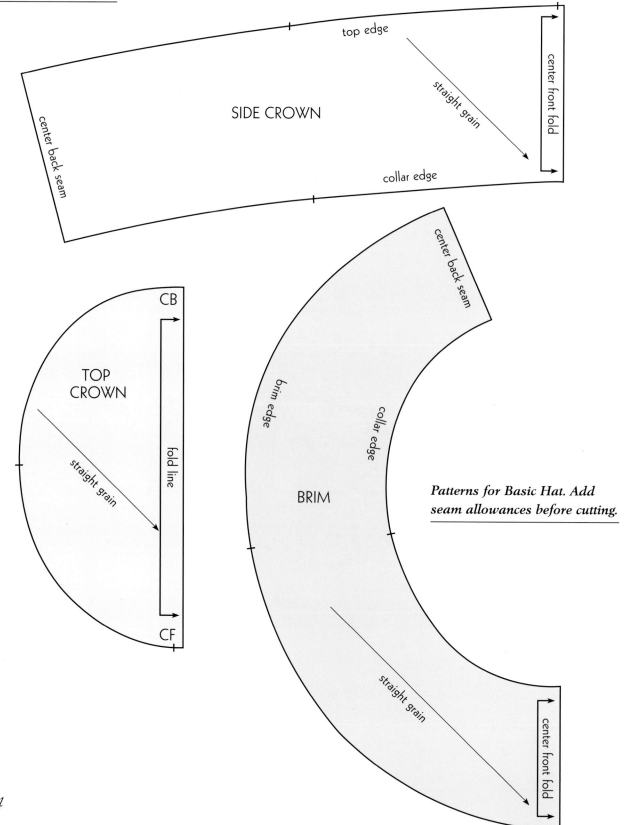

SIDE CROWN

top edge

straight grain

center front fold

center back seam

collar edge

TOP CROWN

CB

fold line

straight grain

CF

center back seam

brim edge

collar edge

BRIM

straight grain

center front fold

Patterns for Basic Hat. Add seam allowances before cutting.

Ascot

The side crown of this design is slightly shorter and not as straight as the crown of the Basic Hat. The brim is the basic brim extended in width; it can be turned up to one side. To make the brim wider, simply add some width to the brim edge of the pattern. How much to add depends on the hat size, anything from 3/8 inch to 2 inches (1 cm to 5 cm).

Materials

✂ Fashion fabric

✂ Fusible nonwoven iron-on interfacing

✂ Batting (wadding)

✂ Lightweight lining fabric such as taffeta

✂ Fine cord for piping*

✂ Contrasting color fabric for making piping*

✂ Decorative cord for the lining (optional)

✂ Materials for pattern making (see Pattern chapter)

Piping is optional.

Pieces to Cut

Fashion fabric + interfacing: 1 side crown, 1 top crown, and 2 brims (1R)

Lining: 1 side crown and 1 top crown

Batting (wadding): 1 brim, 1 side crown, and 1 top crown

The order of work for Ascot is the same as for the Basic Hat. Follow the Basic Hat instructions to make the Ascot.

Two hats made with the Ascot pattern. Left, floral with yellow piped top crown and rouleau trim. Right, red silk with floral flower trim.

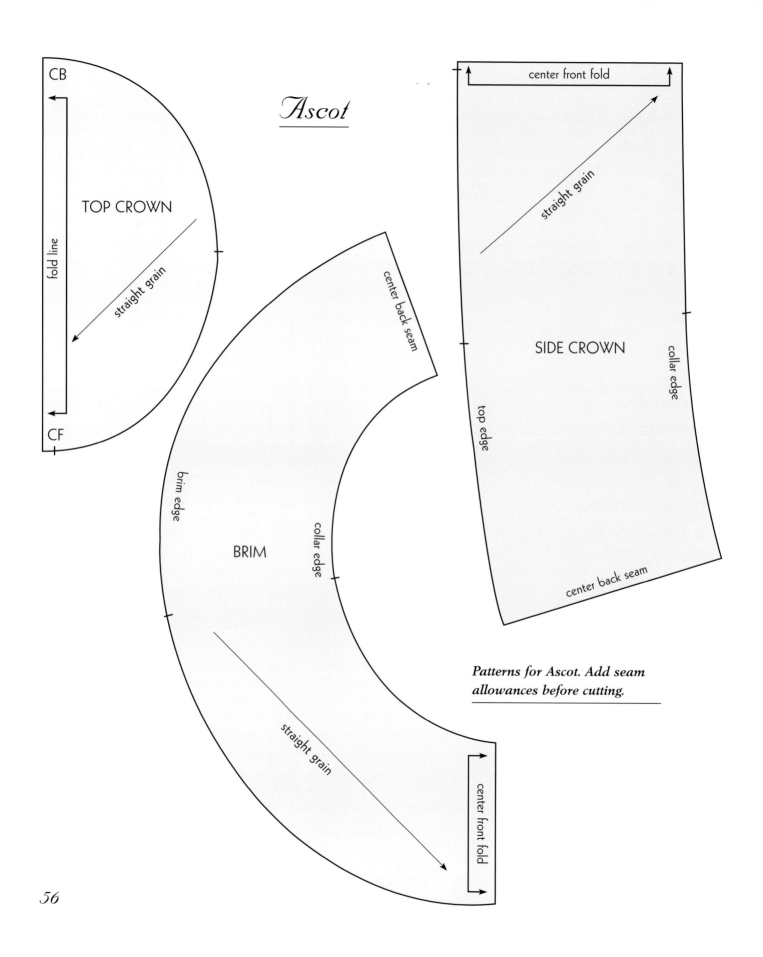

Ascot

CB

TOP CROWN

fold line

straight grain

CF

center back seam

brim edge

BRIM

collar edge

straight grain

center front fold

straight grain

SIDE CROWN

top edge

collar edge

center back seam

center front fold

Patterns for Ascot. Add seam allowances before cutting.

56

Race Day

The side crown is wider at the top edge than at the bottom edge. The brim can be turned up slightly, all around the outer edge, or to one side. To make the brim wider, simply add some width to the brim edge of the pattern. How much depends on the hat size, anything from ⅜ inch to 2 inches (1 cm to 5 cm).

Hats made with Race Day pattern. Left, blue silk with topstitched brim and black fabric bow. Middle, cream silk decorated with tulle and fabric roses. Right, fuchsia hat with black and gold tulle trim.

Materials

✂ Fashion fabric

✂ Fusible nonwoven iron-on inter-facing

✂ Batting (wadding)

✂ Lightweight lining fabric such as taffeta

✂ Fine cord for piping*

✂ Contrasting color fabric for making piping*

✂ Decorative cord for the lining (optional)

✂ Materials for pattern making (see Pattern chapter)

*Piping is optional.

Race Day

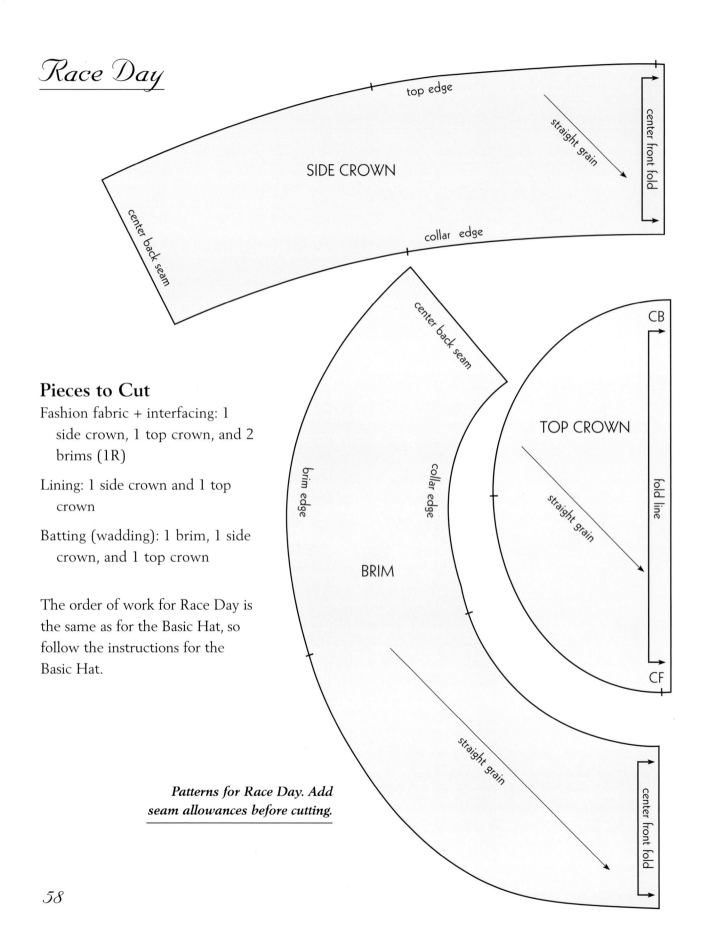

SIDE CROWN

top edge

straight grain

center front fold

center back seam

collar edge

center back seam

brim edge

collar edge

BRIM

straight grain

TOP CROWN

CB

fold line

straight grain

CF

straight grain

center front fold

Pieces to Cut

Fashion fabric + interfacing: 1 side crown, 1 top crown, and 2 brims (1R)

Lining: 1 side crown and 1 top crown

Batting (wadding): 1 brim, 1 side crown, and 1 top crown

The order of work for Race Day is the same as for the Basic Hat, so follow the instructions for the Basic Hat.

Patterns for Race Day. Add seam allowances before cutting.

Easter Parade

This is a very flamboyant style. The brim and side crown pattern pieces are asymmetrical. The brim turns up to one side and the side crown is shaped to enhance the brim shape. It is important that care be taken when cutting the side crown. The pattern as outlined is for the brim to turn up on the right side. For a left side turnup, simply turn the pattern over before cutting fabric.

Two versions of the Easter Parade hat. Left, in orange silk, with cream tulle and roses for a trim. Right, in cream silk, with a soft orange organdie bow and roses for a trim.

Materials

✂ Fashion fabric, 18 x 45 inches (45 × 115 cm)

✂ Fusible nonwoven iron-on interfacing

✂ Batting (wadding)

✂ Lightweight lining fabric such as taffeta

✂ Contrasting color fabric for making piping*

✂ Fine cord for piping*

✂ Materials for pattern making (see Pattern chapter)

Piping is optional.

Tracing the Patterns

For the patterns to fit within the format of the book, it has been necessary to divide the brim pattern into 2 parts and the side crown into 2 parts. Join the pattern parts before cutting fabric.

1. To trace the brim pattern onto paper, take a large piece of tracing paper and draw a line down the center. Aligning the center front line on the line you drew, trace the outline of the right brim onto the right side of the paper. Be sure to mark the match line. Then align the edge of the traced center front line with the same line on the left brim pattern. Trace the left brim pattern on the left side of the tracing paper, aligning the match lines. Add seam allowances, mark notches, and cut out the whole pattern from paper.

2. To trace the side crown pattern, follow the same method.

Pieces to Cut

Fashion fabric + interfacing: 1 side crown, 1 top crown, and 2 brims (1R)

Lining: 1 side crown and 1 top crown

Batting (wadding): 1 brim, 1 side crown, and 1 top crown

Photo 1. Closeup of brim for Easter Parade shows asymmetrical shape.

Sewing

The order of work for Easter Parade is the same as for the Basic Hat. Follow the instructions for the Basic Hat. Because the brim is an odd shape, when stitching the brim, there will be uneven shapes at the collar edge (Photo 1).

Easter Parade

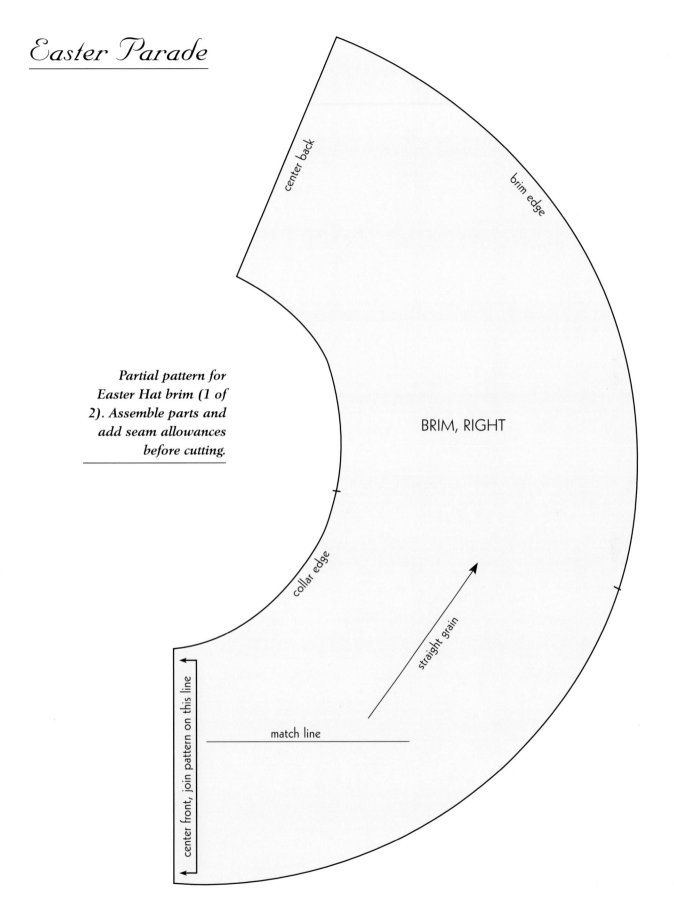

Partial pattern for Easter Hat brim (1 of 2). Assemble parts and add seam allowances before cutting.

center back

brim edge

BRIM, RIGHT

collar edge

straight grain

match line

center front, join pattern on this line

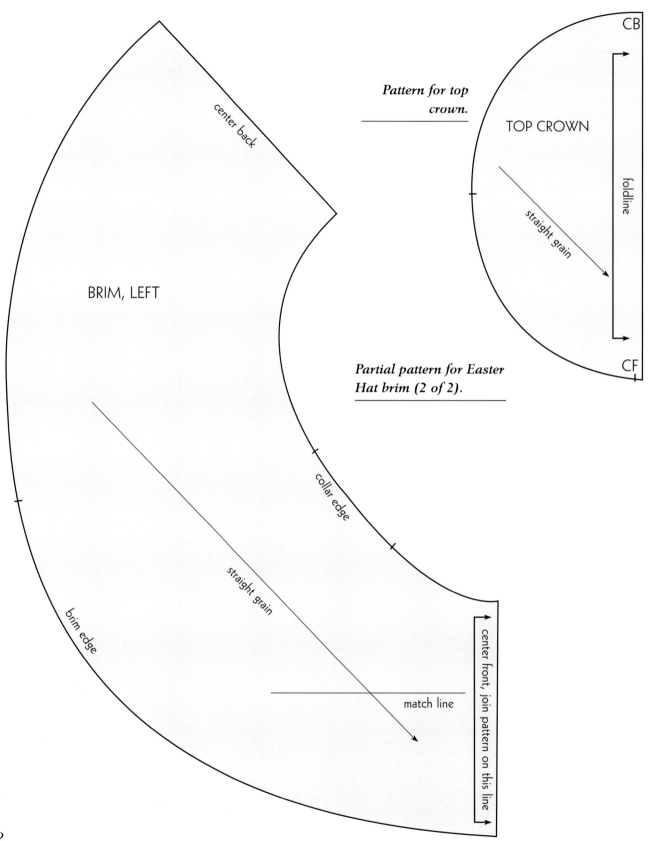

center back

BRIM, LEFT

straight grain

brim edge

match line

collar edge

center front, join pattern on this line

Pattern for top crown.

TOP CROWN

CB

foldline

straight grain

CF

Partial pattern for Easter Hat brim (2 of 2).

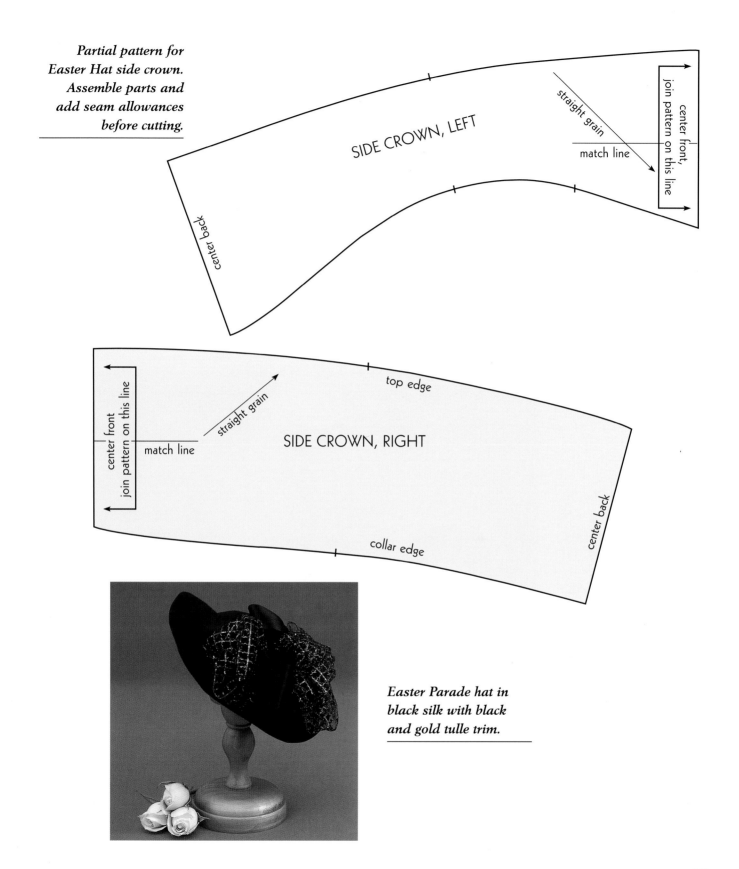

Partial pattern for Easter Hat side crown. Assemble parts and add seam allowances before cutting.

SIDE CROWN, LEFT

straight grain

match line

center front, join pattern on this line

center back

center front, join pattern on this line

match line

straight grain

SIDE CROWN, RIGHT

top edge

center back

collar edge

Easter Parade hat in black silk with black and gold tulle trim.

Boater

The side crown is short and straight at the side. The brim is flat and an even width all around. This brim cannot be turned up. You can use this pattern to create a bridal hat. Attach a tulle veil to the back of the side crown. Hand-sew the lining into the side crown to cover the untidy edges of the tulle.

Hats made with Boater pattern. Left, black fabric Boater with mauve roses. Middle, bridal hat made with brimless Boater and tulle veil. Right, mauve satin Boater has black velvet flowers and mauve hat net veil.

Materials

✀ Fashion fabric

✀ Fusible nonwoven iron-on interfacing

✀ Batting (wadding)

✀ Lightweight lining fabric such as taffeta

✀ Fine cord for piping*

✀ Contrasting color fabric for making piping*

✀ For bridal hat: piece of tulle for veil (optional)

✀ Materials for pattern making (see Pattern chapter)

Piping is optional.

Pieces to Cut

Fashion fabric + interfacing: 1 side crown, 1 top crown, and 2 brims (1R)

Lining: 1 side crown and 1 top crown

Batting (wadding): 1 brim, 1 side crown, and 1 top crown

The order of work for the Boater is the same as for the Basic Hat. Follow the Basic Hat instructions.

Left, black velvet Boater has mauve roses as trim. Right, mauve satin Boater has black velvet flowers and mauve hat net veil.

Boater

Tartan plaid Boater has yellow piped top crown and bow trim.

CB

TOP CROWN

front fold

straight grain

CF

center back seam

BRIM

top edge

center back seam

SHORT SIDE CROWN

straight grain

center front fold

collar edge

top edge

center back seam

ORIGINAL SIDE CROWN

straight grain

center front fold

collar edge

collar edge

straight grain

brim edge

center front fold

Patterns for Boater. Add seam allowances before cutting.

Top Hat

This design has a high, straight side crown. The finished hat has a slightly turned up brim. The brim is a little wider on the sides than that of the Basic Hat on both outside edges. We have given you a choice of two side crown patterns. One is taller than the other. Choose whichever you like.

Materials

✂ Fashion fabric

✂ Fusible nonwoven iron-on interfacing

✂ Batting (wadding)

✂ Lightweight lining fabric such as taffeta

✂ Decorative cord for the lining (optional)

✂ Fine cord for piping*

✂ Contrasting color fabric for making piping*

✂ Materials for pattern making (see Pattern chapter)

Piping is optional.

Pieces to Cut

Fashion fabric + interfacing: 1 side crown, 1 top crown, and 2 brims (1R)

Lining: 1 side crown and 1 top crown

Batting (wadding): 1 brim, 1 side crown, and 1 top crown

Hats made with the Top Hat pattern. Center rear, made of hessian with gold-piped top crown and sunflower trim. Right, blue silk with matching net trim. Front, black velvet with black silk bow trim. Left, leopard print with gold piped top crown and feather trim.

The order of work for the Top Hat is the same as for the Basic Hat, so follow the instructions for the Basic Hat.

Top Hat

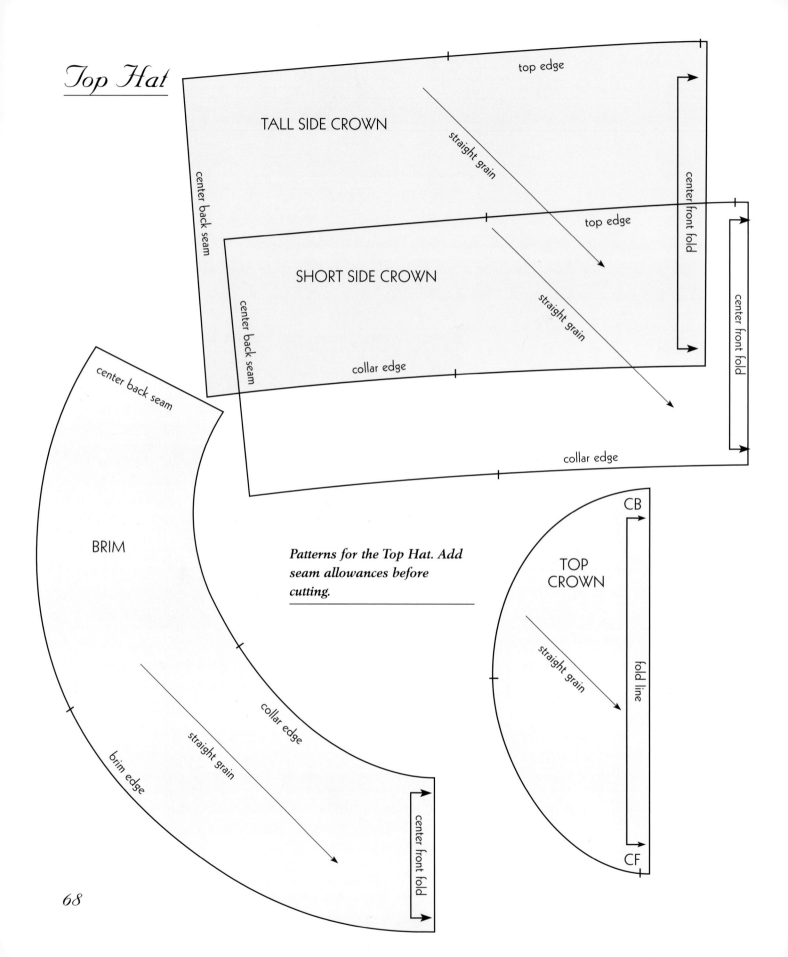

TALL SIDE CROWN

top edge

straight grain

center back seam

center front fold

SHORT SIDE CROWN

top edge

center back seam

straight grain

collar edge

center front fold

collar edge

BRIM

center back seam

straight grain

collar edge

brim edge

straight grain

center front fold

Patterns for the Top Hat. Add seam allowances before cutting.

TOP CROWN

CB

straight grain

fold line

CF

Cloche

The Cloche design has a very close fitting, turned up brim. We have given you two side crown patterns; one is taller than the other. Choose whichever you prefer, or try making some of each height.

Materials

✂ Fashion fabric

✂ Fusible nonwoven iron-on interfacing

✂ Batting (wadding)*

✂ Lightweight lining fabric such as taffeta

✂ Fine cord for piping**

✂ Fabric for piping**

✂ Materials for pattern making (see Pattern chapter)

Depending on the fabric, it is not always necessary to use batting, especially in the small sizes of hat.
**Piping is optional.*

Pieces to Cut

Fashion fabric + interfacing: 1 side crown, 1 top crown, and 2 brims (1R)

Lining: 1 side crown and 1 top crown

Batting (wadding): 1 brim, 1 side crown, and 1 top crown

The order of work for the Cloche is the same as for the Basic Hat, so follow the instructions for the Basic Hat. You may make decorative topstitch lines around the brim or not, as you choose. The brim without topstitching has a softer look. In the examples shown here, the brims have not been stitched.

Hats made from the Cloche pattern: Left, black velvet with black silk bow trim. Center, pink-and-mauve variegated crushed velvet with a mauve bow. Right, green and gold Lurex fabric with a gold bow.

Cloche

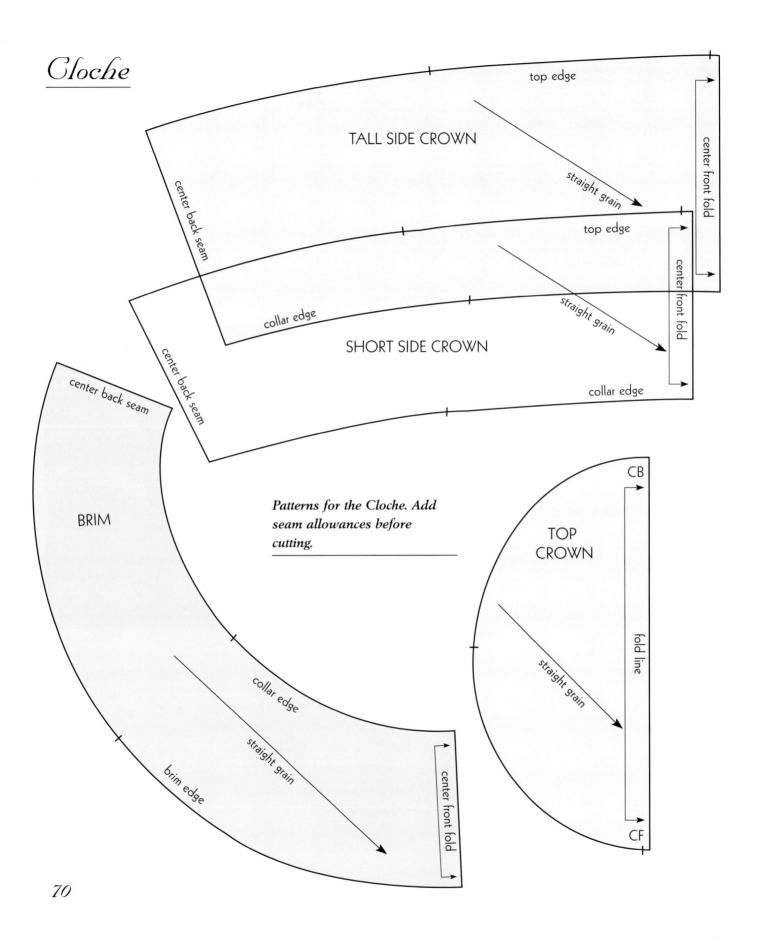

TALL SIDE CROWN

top edge

center front fold

straight grain

center back seam

SHORT SIDE CROWN

top edge

center front fold

collar edge

center back seam

collar edge

center back seam

BRIM

center back seam

Patterns for the Cloche. Add seam allowances before cutting.

collar edge

straight grain

brim edge

center front fold

CB

TOP CROWN

fold line

straight grain

CF

70

Peewee

This is a cute design. The top of the side crown shapes in and the brim can be turned up or down. The crown can be stitched at the top edge to create an outdoors-style hat (see the group photo). For the outdoors style, use fabrics made from natural fibers, such as cotton, silk, or wool. These fibers are more receptive to steaming and shaping, which is important when stitching the top outside edge of the side crown. Before starting the Peewee, read the Basic Hat chapter. The Peewee is made in the same way as the Basic Hat, except for the optional topstitching of the top of the crown. Note: The side crown for the Peewee design is smaller than the top crown by about ⅜ inch or 1 cm.

These hats, made from the Peewee pattern, all have an edge stitched at the top edge of the crown. Left, black velvet fabric; middle, camouflage fabric; right, red-and-green checked fabric.

Materials

✂ Fashion fabric

✂ Fusible nonwoven iron-on interfacing

✂ Batting (wadding)

✂ Lightweight lining fabric such as taffeta

✂ Decorative cord for the lining (optional)

✂ Fine cord for piping*

✂ Contrasting color fabric for making piping*

✂ Materials for pattern making (see Pattern chapter)

Piping is optional.

Pieces to Cut

Fashion fabric + interfacing: 1 side crown, 1 top crown, and 2 brims (1R)

Lining: 1 side crown and 1 top crown

Batting (wadding): 1 brim, 1 side crown, and 1 top crown

Cut out Peewee patterns as for Basic Hat.

Diagram 1. Stitch the top edge of the side crown and top crown together, working with the side crown facing you.

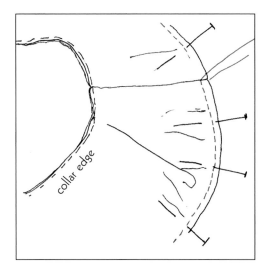

collar edge

Photo 1. Steam the crown unit.

Stitching Together

The order of sewing is the same as for the Basic Hat, so follow the Basic Hat instructions from Directions for Starting through Sewing the Top Crown to the Side Crown, step 8.

Top Stitching Around the Top Crown (optional)

If you want to create a separate edge look at the top of the crown, proceed as follows. This is done before you join the crown unit to the brim.

1. Put a hand inside the side crown and with the other hand finger-press around the seam edge of the side crown towards the top crown.
2. Place the crown down on its collar edge, and steam the top crown to soften the fabric.
3. Finger-press the side crown and the top crown edges together.
4. Pin the fabric together around the top of the top crown, ¼ inch (6 mm) down from the seam edge, working from the side crown side (Diagram 1).
5. Working on the side crown side, stitch the top crown to the side crown, ¼ inch (6 mm) down from the top crown seam line, to create

the raised edge. This can be a bit tricky, so stitch slowly, keeping the seam edge even. With your fingers, ease the side crown into the top crown.

6. Steam the top edge of the side crown (Photo 1).

7. Finger-press the side crown into shape (Photo 2).

8. Place a towel over your hand to protect you from steam, and place your hand inside the crown (Photo 3). Gently press the side crown to the required shape (Photo 3a). Repeat the process until crown is the required shape.

Photo 4 shows the difficulty of sewing the design with synthetic fabric.

Photo 2

Photo 3

Photo 2. Finger-press the crown unit.

Photo 3. Put the crown unit on towel over your hand before steaming.

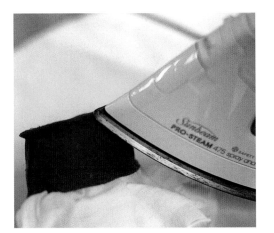

Photo 3a

Photo 4

Photo 3a. With a towel over your hand for protection, gently press the crown into shape.

Photo 4. Here you see the difficulty of sewing synthetic fabrics.

Photo 5. Hold the steam iron over, not on, the brim edge, letting the steam penetrate the brim.

Photo 6. Shape the brim with your fingers.

Photo 7. The finished hat.

Brim

Stitch as for the Basic Hat (see the section on Sewing the Brim). Stitch the crown unit and the brim together as described in the Basic Hat, Joining the Crown Unit to the Brim.

Finishing

1. Rest the brim of the completed hat on the ironing surface. Turn it so the hat is sitting with the top up. Hold the steam iron over, not on, the brim edge, letting the steam penetrate the brim (Photo 5).
2. Shape the brim with your fingers (Photo 6).
3. Line the hat as described in the Basic Hat section on Lining.

Photo 7 shows finished hat.

Peewee

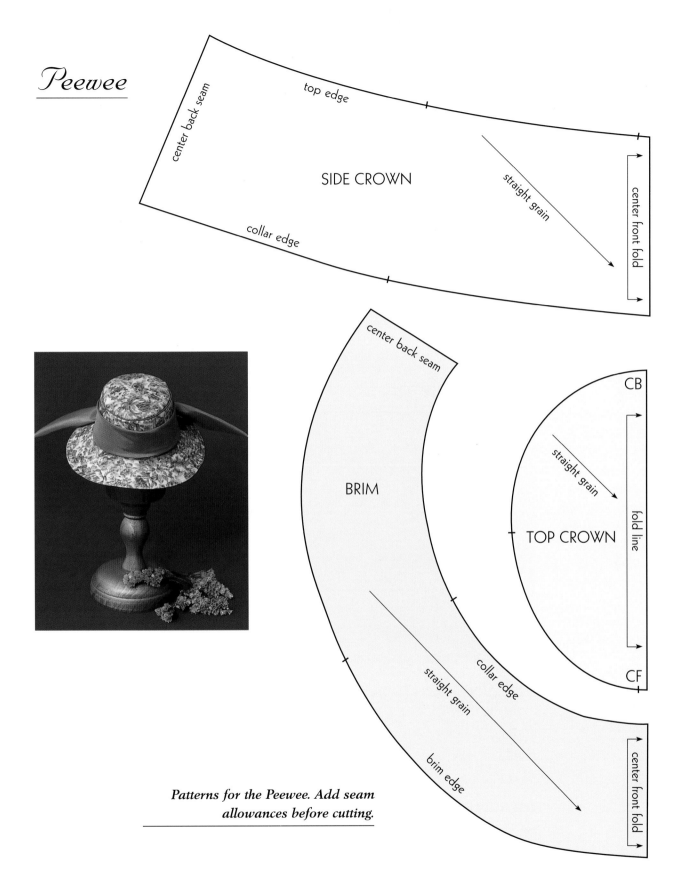

SIDE CROWN

center back seam

top edge

straight grain

center front fold

collar edge

center back seam

BRIM

straight grain

collar edge

brim edge

straight grain

center front fold

CB

TOP CROWN

straight grain

fold line

CF

Patterns for the Peewee. Add seam
allowances before cutting.

Basic Beret

This is a basic beret design, which can made with or without a peak. Piping is optional. Combining the head band and the peak gives a cute military cap. Before starting the Basic Beret, read through the Basic Hat project.

Group of hats made with the Basic Beret pattern. Left rear: navy with peak, gold piping, and gold ricrac braid trim. Center: gold sequin fabric beret. Right: white linen with peak and gold piping trim. Right front: navy with peak and navy and white checked piping trim. Left front: navy and purple crushed velvet beret.

Materials

✄ Fashion fabric

✄ Fusible nonwoven iron-on interfacing

✄ Batting (wadding)

✄ Lightweight lining fabric such as taffeta

✄ Decorative cord for the lining (optional)

✄ Fine cord for piping*

✄ Contrasting color fabric for making piping*

✄ Materials for pattern making (see Pattern chapter)

Piping is optional.

Fuse the fashion fabric to the inter-facing; see the basic instructions chapter for details.

Pieces to Cut*

Fashion fabric + interfacing: 1 under beret, 1 top beret, 2 head bands (1R), 2 peaks (1R)

Lining: 1 under beret, 1 top beret, 1 head band

Batting (wadding): 1 peak

Patterns on page 82.

Stitching Together
Under Beret, Band, Piping

1. Stitch the center back seam of the under beret, with a ⅜ inch (1 cm) seam allowance.
2. Peel the interfacing away from the center back seam allowance, and trim the interfacing back to the stitching.
3. Finger-press the seam allowances flat.
4. Clip off the corners of each of the seam allowances at the ends.
5. Piping is optional. Refer to the Piping chapter before beginning. If the head band is to be piped on both sides, do so now.
6. Pipe the collar edge of the under beret, then the peak edge of the

Navy military style cap made with Basic Beret pattern.

head band. This gives the appearance that the band is piped on both sides (Photo 1 shows piped edges of the head band and under beret).

7. Stitch piping to the top edge of the under beret. Skip to Step 11 if you are not adding a peak.

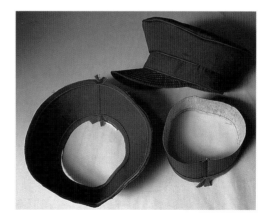

Photo 1. Piped lower edges of head band and under beret.

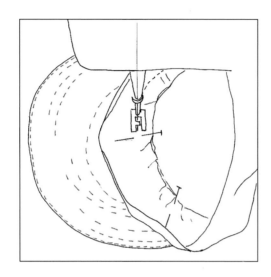

Diagram 1. Stitching the peak to the head band at the center front.

Photo 2. Joining the peak and the head band.

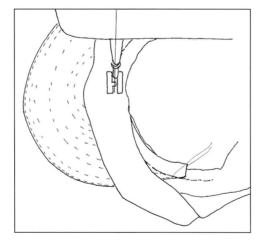

Diagram 2. Stitching on the second head band section.

8. To make the peak, first read the Peak section on page 94. Make the peak and stitch it to the peak edge of the head band (Diagram 1, Photo 2), in the method described in the Peak chapter.

9. Stitch the second head band onto the peak + head band unit, encasing the peak between the two (Diagram 2).

10. Carefully clip, at an angle, the collar edge of the peak only, every ⅜ inch (1 cm) to very close to the stitching line, ⅛ inch (2 mm) away. (You can see clipping in Photo 2 of Country Cap.)

11. If you aren't adding a peak, stitch the 2 head bands together on the peak edge.

12. Edge-stitch the underside seam of the band (Diagram 3). This enables the band to sit firmly up into the inside (Diagram 3a).

13. Stitch the head bands together at the collar edge (Diagram 4). This makes it easier to stitch the head band to the collar edge of the under beret.

Top Beret to Under Beret

To attach the top beret to the under beret, follow the same procedure as is given in the Basic Hat for attaching the top crown to the side crown.

1. Turn the under beret inside out, set the top beret inside, right side to right side; align the notches and pin, first at the center back, then at the center front, then at each side.

2. Stitch on the under beret at the side, starting stitching ⅜ inch (1 cm) before the center back seam. As you stitch, slightly ease the edge of the under beret, keeping this edge in line with the curve of the top beret.

3. Continue sewing around the top edge of the under beret and over-stitch ⅜ inch (1 cm) over the beginning stitches.

4. Trim the interfacing back to the stitching in the same manner as for the Basic Hat.

5. Turn the beret through to the right side. Hold the steam iron over the inside of the beret, fill it with steam, and finger-press the beret into shape.

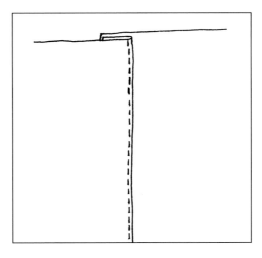

Diagram 3. Edge stitching the under side seam of the band.

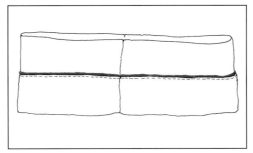

Diagram 3a. The piped band with edge stitching.

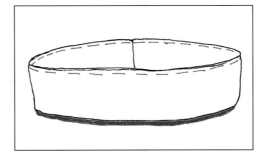

Diagram 4. Stitch the head bands together at the collar edge.

Photo 3. Fold the band to the right side of the beret.

Photo 4. Assembled lining pinned to the fabric beret.

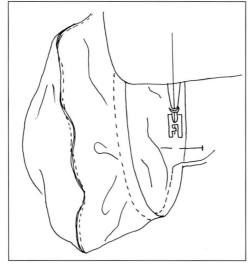

Diagram 5. Stitching the lining to the fashion fabric beret.

6. Pin the head band to the under beret, aligning notches at the center back, center front, and sides. Stitch together on the collar edge of the under beret.

Lining

1. Stitch the top beret and the under beret of the lining together as you did for the fashion fabric of the beret. Start stitching at the center front notch of the under beret.
2. Fold the head band to the right side of the beret toward the top edge (Photo 3).
3. Place the assembled lining over the fabric beret, right sides together. Pin together, aligning notches at the center back, center front and sides (Photo 4).
4. Stitch the lining and the fabric beret from the interfacing side of the beret (Diagram 5), starting ⅜ inch (1 cm) before the center back seam.

5. On the lining side, unpick the seam stitching approximately ¾ inch (2 cm) at either side of the center front notch (Diagram 6).

6. Pull the right side of the fabric beret through the seam opening.

7. With a hand sewing needle, slipstitch the seam opening together.

8. Steam the inside of beret and finger-press into shape.

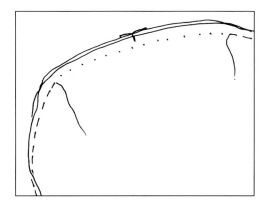

Diagram 6. Unpick part of the seam stitching on the lining side.

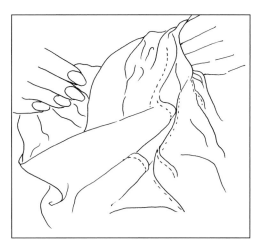

Diagram 7. Pull the fabric beret through the seam opening.

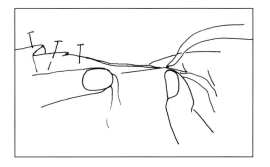

Diagram 8. Slipstitch the seam opening closed.

Basic Beret

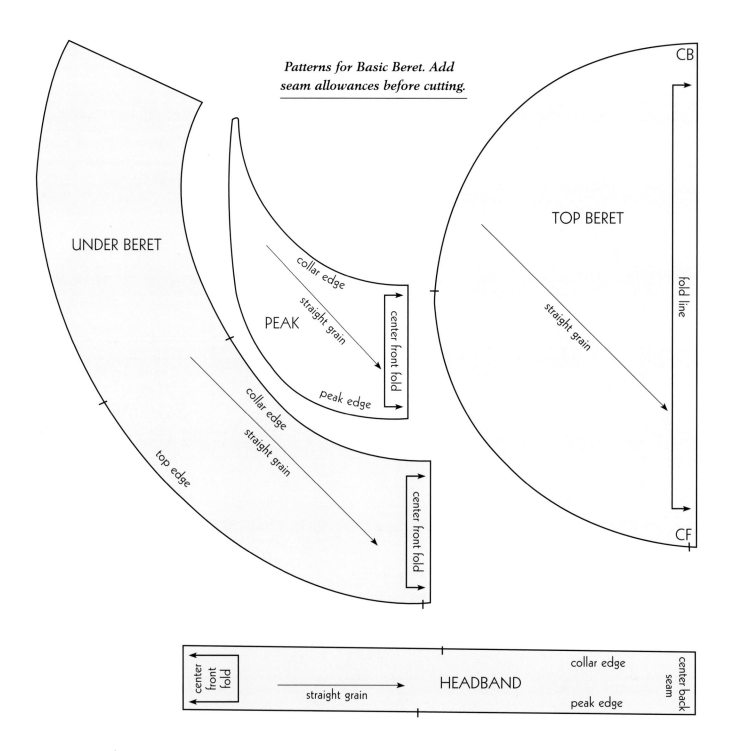

Patterns for Basic Beret. Add
seam allowances before cutting.

TOP BERET

CB

CF

fold line

straight grain

UNDER BERET

PEAK

collar edge

straight grain

center front fold

peak edge

collar edge

straight grain

top edge

center front fold

HEADBAND

center front fold

straight grain

collar edge

peak edge

center back seam

Chef's Hat

Use the side crown pattern of the Top Hat, with a circle of fabric sewn to the top edge of the side crown for the rounded top (blouson), to create the Chef's Hat.

Hats from the Chef's Hat pattern. Left, made with Christmas print; center, red and white checks; right, white linen.

Materials

✄ Fashion fabric

✄ Fusible nonwoven iron-on interfacing

✄ Lightweight lining fabric such as taffeta

✄ Materials for pattern making (see Pattern chapter)

Pieces to Cut

From fabric + interfacing: cut 1 side crown

From lining fabric: cut 1 side crown

From fabric alone: cut 1 circle. Use the quarter-circle pattern (p. 87) to cut the rounded top of the hat. Trace this pattern onto tracing

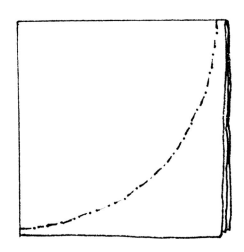

Diagram 1. Place the paper pattern quarter circle on fabric folded in quarters.

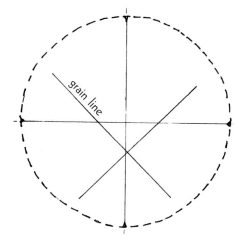

grain line

Diagram 2. Mark and clip notches on the fabric's folds.

paper and place it on a piece of fabric that has been folded in quarters, aligning the foldlines (Diagram 1). Mark and clip notches with a water-soluble pen on the edge of the circle at the folds (Diagram 2).

Sewing

1. Using a normal stitch length, sew the back seam of the side crown of the fabric + interfacing and sew the back seam of the lining side crown, with ⅜ inch (1 cm) seam allowances.

2. Peel the interfacing away from the center back seam allowance of the fabric + interfacing side crown, and trim back the interfacing to the stitching line.

3. Clip off the ends of the seam allowances of the side crowns. Finger-press seam allowances open.

4. At the collar edge, pin the lining side crown and the fabric + interfacing side crown together, with right sides facing. With a normal stitch length, sew the two together, starting ⅜ inch (1 cm) before the center back seam, continuing around, and overstitching ⅜ inch beyond the starting point. Edge-

stitch the collar edge seam from the lining side. This enables the lining to sit firmly up into the side crown.

5. Turn the joined side crowns right-side out. Using a long machine stitch and aligning notches of lining and fabric side crown at the top edge, stitch the lining side crown to the fabric side crown at the top edge. This will make sewing the gathered rounded top to the side crown easier (Diagram 3).

6. Using a long machine stitch, starting at the center back notch, sew a line of stitches around the edge of the circle of the hat top along the seam line to use as a gathering thread (Diagram 4). Tie a knot in one end of the threads.

7. Turn the side crown of the Chef's Hat so the lining is facing out; then pin the circle inside, with the right side of fabric facing the fashion fabric of the side crown, aligning the notches of the circle with the notches on the top edge of the side crown. Pull the gathering thread, gathering the top circle to fit the side crown. Pin the gathers in place for stitching, or baste.

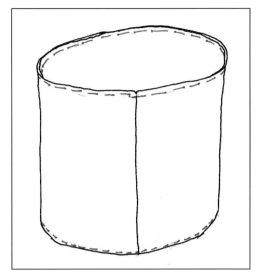

Diagram 3. The lining and fabric + interfacing side crowns stitched together.

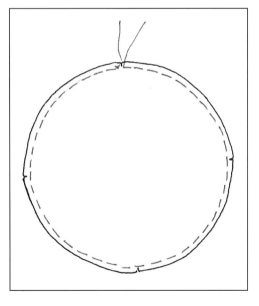

Diagram 4. Machine-stitch gathering thread around the fabric circle.

Diagram 5. Stitch the rounded top to the side crown.

Photo 1. Side crown with lining side out and the round top stitched in place.

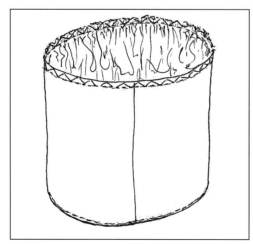

Diagram 5

Diagram 6. Tidy the top seam with zigzag stitching.

Diagram 6

Photo 1

8. Stitch the top and side crown together with normal stitch length (Diagram 5, Photo 1).
9. After the two are stitched, zigzag stitch or overlock stitch the edges to make them tidy (Diagram 6).
10. Turn the hat right-side out.

Chef's Hat

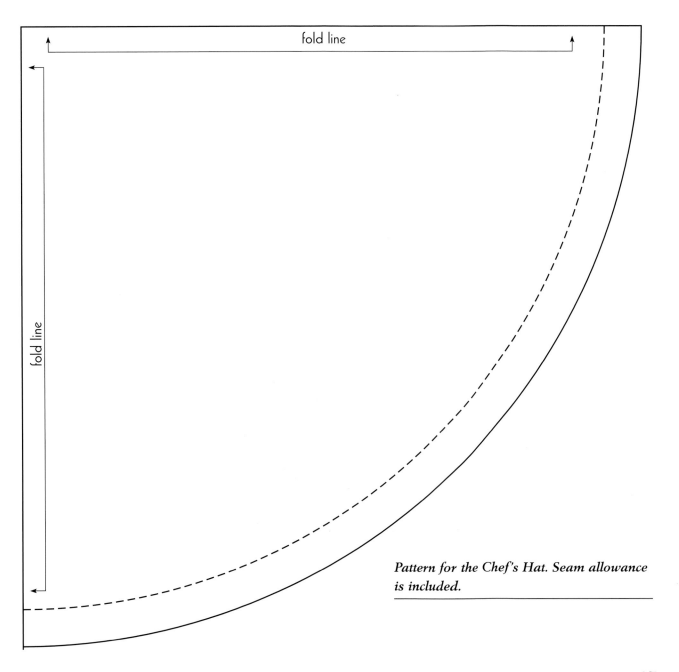

fold line

fold line

Pattern for the Chef's Hat. Seam allowance
is included.

Diagram 1

A piece crown is a crown that is made in sections. The book includes designs for a 3-Piece Crown with peak, a 5-Piece Crown with peak (or brim), and a 6-Piece Beret with or without peak. A brim can be attached to the 5-Piece Crown. The Trilby design is a 4-piece crown.

When attaching a piece crown to a brim, the piece crown should be approximately ⅜ inch (1 cm) larger at the collar edge than the collar edge of brim. This allows the collar edge of the piece crown to have a slight roll over the join to the brim (Diagram 1). If they are the same measurement at the collar edge, the piece crown is taut at the join to the brim and tends to distort the shape of the finished hat.

Group of hats made with Trilby pattern. Left, white linen with black band trim. Center, Lurex fabric with gold band trim. Right, red wool with black band trim.

3-Piece Round Crown

This design has the look of an English country hat. It has a center panel with a half circle on either side. The round crown look can be altered by simply sewing a dart in the top of the center panel.

Hats made from the 3-Piece Round Crown pattern. The left and center hats have darts. The right, a crushed maroon velvet, does not.

Materials

✄ Fashion fabric

✄ Fusible nonwoven iron-on interfacing

✄ Batting (wadding)

✄ Lightweight lining fabric such as taffeta

✄ Materials for pattern making (see Pattern chapter)

See the basic instructions for fusing fabric to interfacing and press the fashion fabric to the fusible iron-on interfacing. Add seam allowances to pattern pieces before cutting.

Pieces to Cut

Fashion fabric + interfacing: 2 side crowns (1R), 1 center panel, 2 brims (1R)

Lining: 2 side crowns (1R), 1 center panel

Batting: 1 brim

Cutting Out and Preparing

Remember to add seam allowances to pattern pieces.

1. Fold the fashion fabric + fusible iron-on interfacing, interfacing side out.
2. Place the brim and side crown pattern in place. Pin carefully and sparingly to avoid distorting shape. Cut out the brim and side crown pieces. Pin the center panel on the bias on one layer of fabric + interfacing and cut out. Pinning the center panel on the bias makes it easier to sew.
3. Cut out the brim pattern in batting. Split the batting pieces, if necessary, to get the proper thickness.

4. Before you remove the pattern pieces from the fabric, clip the notches and mark them with a water-soluble pen.
5. To avoid having the fabric + interfacing pattern pieces coming apart while you sew, stitch around the fabric + interfacing side crowns and center panel just inside the cut edge, using your longest machine stitch.

Stitching the Crown

All construction is done with right sides together, unless noted.

1. Pin the center panel of fashion fabric + interfacing to one of the side crowns on the curved edges all the way around the curve, pinning at notches.
2. With a normal stitch length, with the center panel facing up, start at a collar edge and stitch the center panel and side crown pieces together, all the way around the curve. As you stitch, slightly pull the edge of center panel, keeping this edge in line with the curve of the side crown.

3. Stitch the other side crown to the center panel in the same way (Photo 1).

4. Trim back the interfacing seam allowances to $\frac{1}{16}$ inch (2 mm) from the stitching on the seams you made.

5. Finger-press the seam allowances open.

6. Place a towel over your hand to protect it from the steam; then place your hand inside the crown. Gently press the seams with the steam iron (see Diagram 1).

7. If you want a dip or valley in the center panel, fold the crown in half, down the center of the center panel, and mark a dart on the center panel as indicated on the pattern. Stitch the dart in the center of the center panel. The widest part of the dart is in line with the notch at the center of the panel.

Photo 1. Stitching the side crown to the center panel of the 3-Piece Round Crown. Stitch from the center panel side, pulling the edge slightly to align with the curve of the side crown.

Diagram 1. Cover your hand with a towel and gently press the seams with a steam iron.

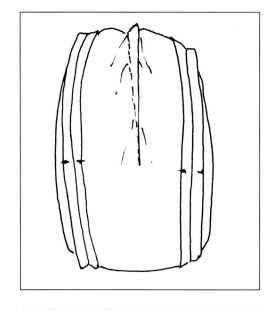

Diagram 2. The stitched center dart, with the crown inside out.

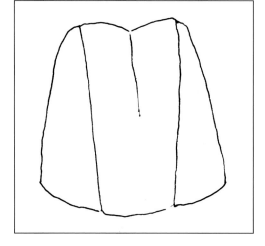

Diagram 3. The stitched center dart, with the crown right-side out.

Diagram 2 and Diagram 3 illustrate the shape of the crown with the dart.

8. Using a long machine stitch, stitch a gathering line around the collar edge of the crown, just inside the seam allowance. Pulling this thread will enable you to pull in the extra fullness, making it easier to fit the crown and the brim.

9. Stitch and attach the brim in the same manner as for the brim of the Basic Hat.

10. See the Basic Hat instructions for lining directions.

3-Piece Round Crown

Patterns for the 3-Piece Round Crown.
Add seam allowances before cutting.

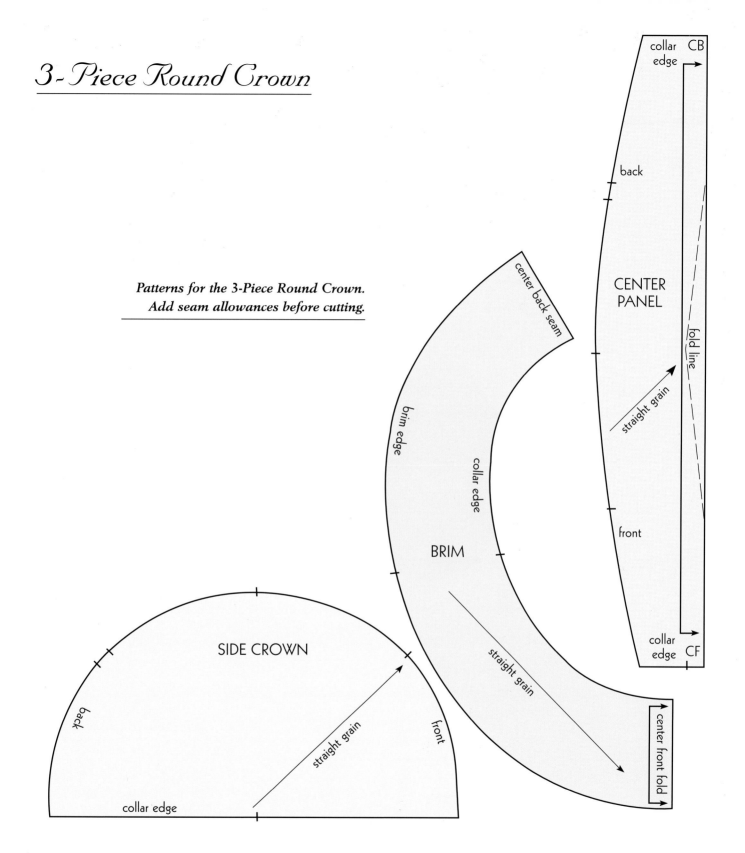

collar edge

CB

back

CENTER PANEL

fold line

straight grain

front

collar edge

CF

center back seam

brim edge

collar edge

BRIM

straight grain

center front fold

SIDE CROWN

back

front

straight grain

collar edge

The Peak

These instructions can be used for the peak of any hat that has a peak. The method of making a peak is similar to that of making a brim, but the shape is different. Topstitching the peak is optional, and may be done in the same color as the fabric or in a contrasting color of thread.

Materials

✄ Fashion fabric

✄ Fusible nonwoven iron-on interfacing

✄ Batting (wadding)

✄ Materials for tracing a pattern (see Pattern chapter)

Pieces to Cut

From fashion fabric + interfacing: 2 peaks (1R)

From batting: 1 peak; split the batting to the required thickness

Remember to add seam allowances before cutting pieces.

Sewing the Peak

1. Using a long machine stitch, stitch the batting peak to one of the fabric + interfacing peak pieces, inside the seam allowances, close to the edges.
2. Pin the second fabric + interfacing peak to the unit made in step 1, with right sides of fabric facing. Using a normal machine stitch length, sew the two pieces together around the outside edge of the peak, leaving the collar edge unsewn. On the brim edge of the peak, unpick the long stitches holding the batting to the peak

fabric and trim back the batting seam allowances to the seam line. Do not trim back at the collar edge of the peak.

3. Turn the peak right-side out.

4. Pin the collar edges of the peak layers together at the notches. Using a long machine stitch, stitch the peak pieces together just inside the collar edge seam allowance (see left in Photo 1 and Diagram 1).

5. Hold the steam iron over, but not on, the peak and allow the steam to penetrate.

6. Finger-press and roll the edge seams of the peak so they are in line.

Topstitching Lines on the Peak (optional)

1. You can use contrasting thread or thread the same color as the fabric. Using a normal stitch length, starting on the outside edge of the peak, as close to the edge as possible, sew a line of stitches around to the other side of the peak.

2. Lift the sewing machine foot and turn the peak. Place the needle about ⅛ inch (4 mm) away from the previous row of stitching, and

Photo 1. To topstitch the peak, start stitching just inside collar edge seam allowance. Right, stitching complete.

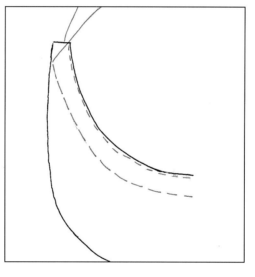

Diagram 1. Stitch the peak just inside the collar edge seam allowance.

continue sewing around the peak edge to the other side (Diagram 2), up to the line of stitching at the collar edge. Turn the peak to enable you to stitch along the stitch line at collar edge, until the distance from the previous curved row of peak is ⅛ inch (4 mm). Then start a new curved row of topstitching, parallel to the first row of topstitching.

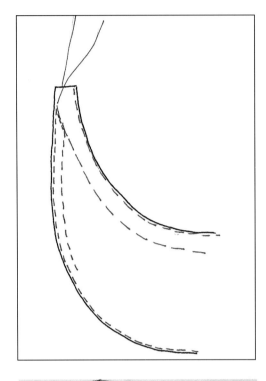

Diagram 2. Start top-stitching the peak near the outer edge.

Photo 2. Detail of stitched peak.

3. Continue to topstitch the peak in this manner (see right in Photo 1, Photo 2, and Diagram 3).

4. Steam press the stitched peak.

Attaching the Peak and the Lining

1. Pin the peak in place on the outside of the fashion fabric hat, matching its center front to the center front of the hat or cap, and matching notches. With some fabrics, it is advisable to stitch a row of long machine stitches just inside the collar edge of the seam allowance of the hat. Tie a knot in one end of the thread and then pull the other end of the thread to slightly gather (ease) the hat to fit the collar edge of the peak, before pinning the peak in place. Starting at one side notch, stitch the peak to the collar edge of the hat.

2. When you stitch the lining to the hat, pin the peak up to the front side of the hat so it is out of the way. The cap should be right-side out. Place the lining over the cap, with right sides of fabric facing each other. Align the notches at the collar edge. Using a normal stitch length, starting ⅜ inch (1 cm) before the center back, sew the lining to the hat at the collar edge; overstitch your stitches at the starting point by ⅜ inch.

3. When the lining has been stitched onto the hat, clip off the peak tails that extend beyond the seam line to reduce bulk (Photo 3).

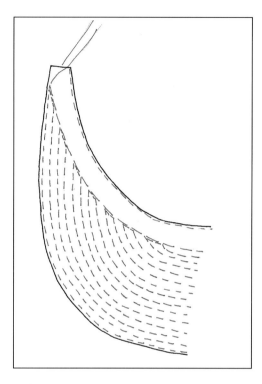

Diagram 3. The top-stitched peak.

Photo 3. Clip off the peak's "tails."

Sports Cap

The Sports Cap has a 3-piece crown. It is meant to have a peak and is not suitable for combining with a brim. It has a cutout in the back, and the back sections are held together by ribbon or two short ties of rouleau, which may be made in the same fabric as the hat.

Group of piece caps includes 3-piece Sports Caps in red fabric with gold piping and trim; in navy with rooster trim; and in green fabric with ABC trim.

Materials

✂ Fashion fabric

✂ Fusible nonwoven iron-on interfacing

✂ Batting (wadding)

✂ Lightweight lining fabric such as taffeta

✂ Cord and fashion fabric for rouleau (optional) or thin ribbon for ties

✂ Materials for pattern making (see Pattern chapter)

Press the fashion fabric to the interfacing (see basic instructions chapter).

Pieces to Cut

Fabric + interfacing: 1 front crown, 2 back crowns (1R), and 2 peaks (1R)

Lining: 1 front crown, 2 back crowns (1R)

Batting: 1 peak; split batting if necessary

Note: Remember to add seam allowances to paper patterns and to clip and mark the notches when the pieces are cut out.

Sewing the Cap

All construction is done with right sides of fabric facing, unless noted.

1. Take the two back crown pieces of fabric + interfacing, pin them together, and stitch the center back seam with a ¼ inch (6 mm) seam allowance (see Diagram 1).
2. Trim back the interfacing seam allowance to the stitching line on the stitched edges (Diagram 2).
3. Pin the front crown to the back crown unit, matching the notches.
4. Starting at the top, stitch to the

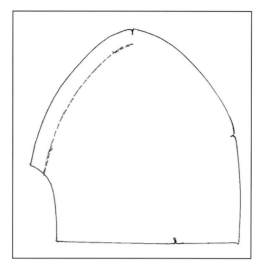

Diagram 1. Stitch the two back crown sections together along the center back seam.

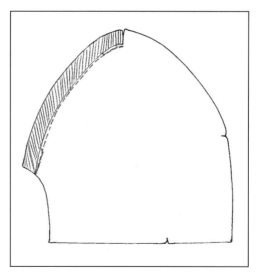

Diagram 2. Trim back the fusible interfacing to the stitching line on the seam just stitched.

Photo 1. Left, front crown is stitched to a back crown section. On the right, the interfacing seam allowance has been trimmed back.

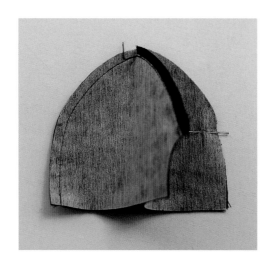

Diagram 3. Stitch the front to the back unit along one seam.

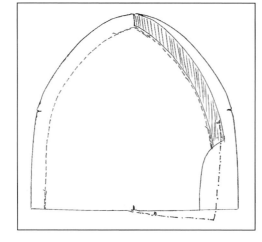

collar edge on one side seam with a ¼ inch (6 mm) seam allowance (Photo 1, left, Diagram 3), reverse stitch for ⅜ inch (1 cm), and cut off the thread tails. Repeat for the second side seam.

5. Trim back the interfacing on the stitched seam allowances to the stitching line.

6. Finger-press the seams open.

7. Place a towel over the hand, place the hand inside the crown, hold the steam iron over seam, and lightly press the seam with the tip of the iron (see Trilby chapter, Photo 2, for steaming).

8. Sew the lining front and back crown together in the same way you stitched the fashion fabric pieces.

9. For ties at the back opening of the hat, use ribbons or make two rouleau cords from the fashion fabric of about 4 inches (10 cm) in length each. Topstitch one tie to the right side of each back crown fashion fabric section, ¼ inch (6 mm) up from the collar edge and ¼ inch (6 mm) in from the curved edge (Photo 2).

10. Make the peak and stitch it on the front of the cap as described in the Peak chapter.

11. Pin the lining unit with its right side facing the right side of the fashion fabric hat, being careful to tuck the peak up out of the way during stitching. Start stitching the lining and fashion fabric together on the collar edge, 1 inch (2.5 cm) from the center back opening (Photo 3).

Photo 2. Stitch the ties in place on the right side of the back crown fashion fabric, about ¼ inch (.5 cm) above the collar edge seam allowance.

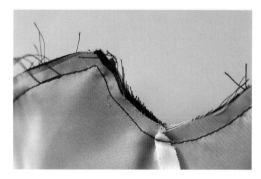

Photo 3. Stitching the lining to the fashion fabric at the center back opening.

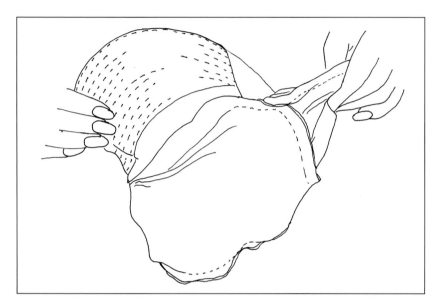

Diagram 4. Pull the fabric cap through the opening in lining.

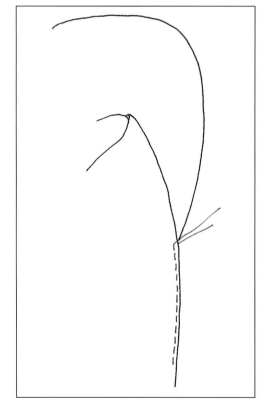

Diagram 5. Stitch the edge of cap starting from the side of one of the peak edges.

12. On the lining side, unpick a section of stitching a few inches long at one of the seams. Pull the cap through the opening in the lining and turn to the right side (Diagram 4). Hand stitch the lining together.

13. To keep the collar edge flat, working from the fashion fabric side of the collar edge, beginning next to one edge of the peak, stitch close to the edge, around to the far edge of the peak (Diagram 5).

14. Steam the cap to shape it.

Sports Cap

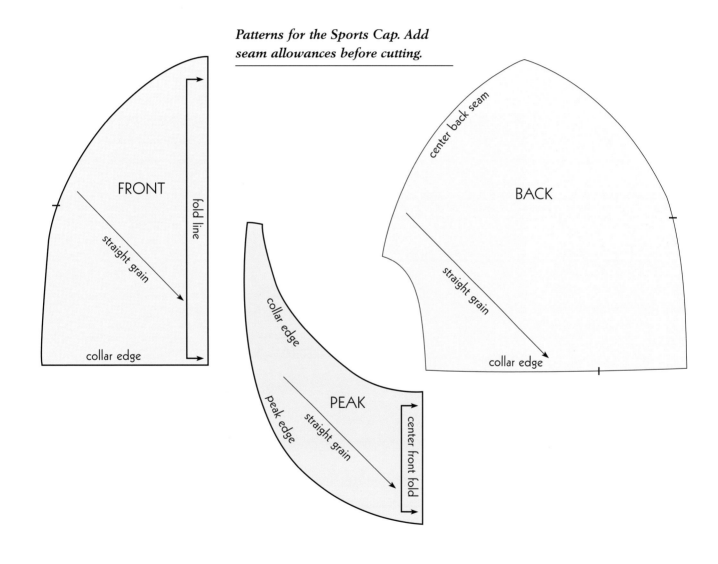

Patterns for the Sports Cap. Add seam allowances before cutting.

FRONT

straight grain

fold line

collar edge

PEAK

collar edge

peak edge

straight grain

center front fold

BACK

center back seam

straight grain

collar edge

6-Piece Beret

The crown of this beret is made of 6 sections. You can make the beret using the wider or the narrower section patterns. Both are given here (style 1 and style 2). The beret may be made with or without the peak. For the peak, use the pattern from the 5-Piece Crown chapter (page 111).

Hats made with 6-Piece Beret pattern, with and without the peak. Clockwise from back left, black and green fabric beret, silver fabric beret with peak, red and green check fabric beret with peak, gold and black fabric beret, pink fabric beret.

Fuse the fabric to the interfacing as described in the basics chapter. Section patterns are given as half patterns; make a full pattern on tracing paper before cutting fabric (see the chapter on patterns for details).

Pieces to Cut

Fashion fabric + interfacing: 6 sections and 2 peaks, 1R (optional)

Batting: 1 peak (optional)

Lining: 6 sections

Cutting Instructions

1. Cut 6 pattern pieces in fabric + interfacing; placement on fabric depends on the fabric's design.
2. Cut 6 pattern pieces in lining fabric. Cut 2 peaks from fabric + interfacing and one peak from batting if you are planning a peak. Split the peak batting piece if it is too thick.
3. Clip and mark the notches on all pieces.

Stitching the Beret

All construction is done with right sides of fabric facing unless otherwise noted.

1. Working with 2 sections at a time, align the notches and pin the two sections together from the collar edge to the top point along one side.
2. With a normal stitch length, sew the pinned seam to within ¼ inch (6 mm) of the top point.
3. Trim back the interfacing to the stitching on the seam just sewn (Photo 1).
4. Set the two joined sections aside and repeat steps 1 through 3 for remaining 4 sections.

Multicolored fabric beret with peak, made from 6-Piece Beret pattern.

Photo 1. Sections with fusible interfacing trimmed back to seam allowance.

Photo 2. Press seam allowances open with the tip of an iron.

5. Matching notches, pin two 2-section units together along one side from the collar edge to the top, and stitch as earlier, to make a 4-section unit.

6. Stitch the last 2-section unit to the 4-section unit in the same way; sew it on both side seams. The six pieces are now sewn together. Trim back the interfacing to the seam lines on all stitched edges.

7. Finger-press the seam allowances open.

8. Place a towel over the hand, place the hand inside the crown, hold the steam iron over the seam, and lightly press the seam with the tip of the iron (Photo 2).

9. Sew the lining section pieces to each other in the same way you did for the fabric + interfacing pieces.

The Peak for the 6-Piece Beret (optional)

1. See instructions for making a peak in the basic Peak chapter. The peak is attached before the lining.

2. To attach the peak, position the peak so it centers on whatever part you have chosen for the center front, aligning it either on a seam or on the center fold of a section. When the peak is placed on the center fold of a section, the beret crown tends to sit up. When placed on a seam, it gives a flatter appearance to the beret crown.

Sewing in the Lining

1. Turn the fashion fabric + interfacing beret right side out, and place the lining over this, right side to right side. The wrong side of the lining should be facing you. Align the lining and fashion fabric seams at the collar edge.

2. Using a normal stitch length, stitch all around the edge of the beret at the collar edge, with a ¼ inch (6 mm) seam allowance (Photo 3), starting at the center back. If there is a peak attached, make sure it is tucked up out of the way between the fashion fab-

Photo 3

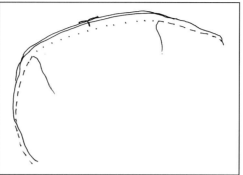

Diagram 1

Photo 3. View of the lining stitched to the fashion fabric beret.

Diagram 1. Unpick some stitching in the lining.

Photo 4

Photo 4. Pull the fabric beret through the hole in lining to turn the beret right-side out.

Photo 5

Photo 5. Once the whole hat is turned right side out, push the lining inside the hat.

ric and the lining while you stitch.

3. On the lining, unpick some of the stitching, about ¾ inch (2 cm) to either side of the middle on one of the seams (Diagram 1). Tie off the thread ends so the seam doesn't open further.

4. Pull the beret through the opening in the seam and push the lining inside the hat (Photos 4 and 5).

Diagram 2. Slipstitch the lining opening closed.

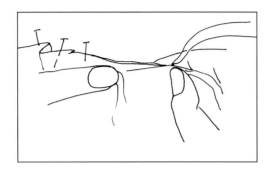

5. With a hand sewing needle, slip-stitch the opened seam closed (Diagram 2).

Photo 6. Fill the inside of the beret with steam.

6. Hold the steam iron over the inside of the beret, letting the steam fill the inside (Photo 6).

Photo 7. Finger-press the beret to shape it.

7. Gently finger-press the beret into shape (Photo 7).

6-Piece Beret

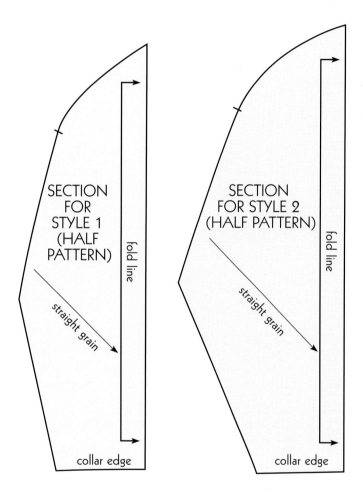

Patterns for the 6-Piece Beret. Add seam allowances before cutting.

5-Piece Crown

This piece crown hat can have a peak, like a jockey cap, or a brim.

Pink sequin fabric hat made with the 5-Piece Crown pattern.

Materials

✄ Fashion fabric

✄ Fusible nonwoven iron-on interfacing

✄ Batting (wadding)

✄ Lightweight lining fabric such as taffeta

✄ Fashion fabric for piping*

✄ Fine cord for piping*

✄ Materials for pattern making (see Pattern chapter)

Piping is optional.

Pieces to Cut

Fashion fabric + interfacing: 5 sections and (optional) 2 peaks (1R), or 2 brims (1R)

Batting: 1 peak (optional)

Lining: 5 sections

For making the peak, see the basic Peak chapter. For the brim, follow the instructions from the Basic Hat chapter. To construct the hat, follow the sewing directions for the 6-Piece Beret, but you will have 5 sections, so you can join them in groups of 2 + 2 + 1.

5-Piece Crown

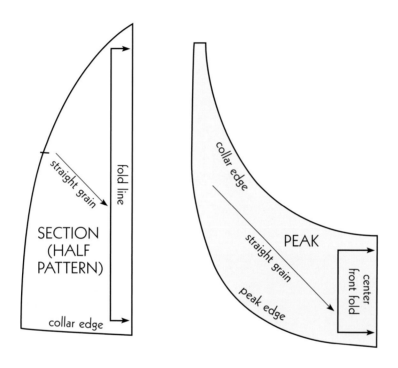

Patterns for the 5-Piece Crown. Add seam allowances before cutting.

Trilby

The Trilby is a 4-piece crown design. The piece crown patterns need to be approximately ⅜ inch (1 cm) larger in total collar edge measurement than the collar measurement of the brim. This enables the crown to roll over at the join of the brim at the collar edge (Diagram 1). If the measurement of the side crown and the brim are the same, the piece crown tends to flatten and pull the design out of shape. The necessary variations in measurement have been allowed for with pattern pieces of this design. If you are joining this piece crown to another brim design, please check the measurements to allow for the difference. For the Trilby design, the crown pieces do not require batting, but the brim does. The amount of fabric + interfacing will depend on whether placement of the patterns is on the straight grain or on the bias.

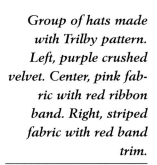

Group of hats made with Trilby pattern. Left, purple crushed velvet. Center, pink fabric with red ribbon band. Right, striped fabric with red band trim.

Materials

✂ Fashion fabric

✂ Fusible nonwoven iron-on interfacing

✂ Batting (wadding)

✂ Lightweight lining fabric such as taffeta

✂ Decorative cord for the lining (optional)

✂ Materials for pattern making (see Pattern chapter)

Pieces to Cut*

Fashion fabric + interfacing:
  2 (1R) of crown section A (front).
  2 (1R) of crown section B (back).
  2 brims (1R)

Lining: 2 of section A (1R) and 2 of section B (1R)

Batting (wadding): 1 brim. Split the batting if needed so it is ¼ inch thick

Patterns on page 117.

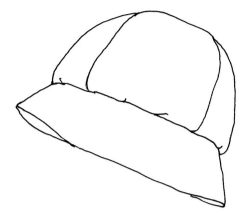

Diagram 1. The necessary roll of the crown over the brim.

Cutting

1. Fuse the fabric to the interfacing as described in the basics section of the book.
2. From folded fabric + interfacing, cut 2 each of crown section A and 2 of B. This gives you the 4 pattern pieces necessary for the Trilby crown. Remember to add seam allowances of ¼ (6 mm) to all pattern pieces before cutting.
3. Clip and mark the notches on the fabric pieces after they are cut out.

Diagram 2. A stitched side seam joins two crown sections.

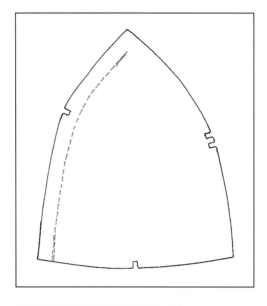

Diagram 3. Trim back the interfacing on the stitched seam allowance to the seam line.

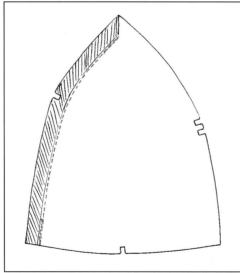

Sewing

The following is the order of sewing for the Trilby. All construction is done with right sides of fabric facing, unless otherwise noted.

1. Take the two A pieces in fabric + interfacing. Pin the side seams (the ones with the single notch) together to within ¼ inch (6 mm) of the point. Then stitch them together on the seam line, using a normal stitch length (Diagram 2), starting at the collar edge.

2. On the edge you just stitched, trim the interfacing back to the stitching line to reduce bulk (Diagram 3).

3. Repeat steps 1 and 2 for the pair of B pieces.

4. Take the units of section A and B. Pin them together, matching double notches, along the center front and center back seam lines. Stitch the center front and center back seams with ¼ inch (6 mm) seam allowances, starting from the collar edge, being careful to keep the top seams in line with each other.

5. Trim interfacing back to the stitching line on the seams just stitched (Photo 1).

6. Cover your hand with a small towel or thick cloth, place it inside the piece crown, and lightly press the seam with the tip of the iron (Photo 2).

7. Using a long machine stitch, stitch around the collar edge of the piece crown, just inside the seam allowance. Pulling this thread will enable the extra fullness to be pulled in, making it easier fitting the crown and the brim.

8. Optional: If you wish, you can edge-stitch (topstitch) the seams of the piece crown at the side seams. Do this from the inside of the piece crown (Photo 3). You can edge-stitch the seams in a color matching the fabric, in which case they are barely seen. Or change to a contrasting color to make the stitching more noticeable. Edge-stitch the side seams first, with your needle 1/32 inch (2 mm) in from the seam

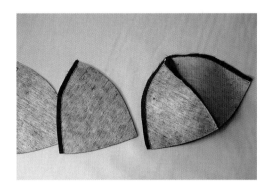

Photo 1. Left: Two sections stitched with interfacing untrimmed. Middle: fusible interfacing trimmed back to stitch line. Right: the four sections stitched and the interfacing trimmed back to the stitch lines.

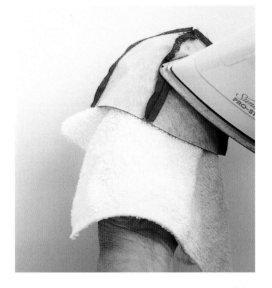

Photo 2. Pressing the seam allowances with the tip of an iron.

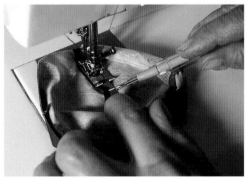

Photo 3. Edge stitching next to the seam line from inside the crown.

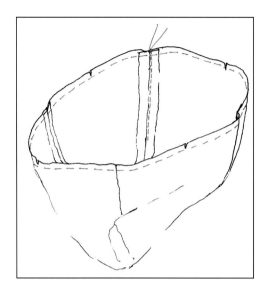

Diagram 4. How the edge stitching looks (dashed line on seam allowance) at the start of stitching inside the crown.

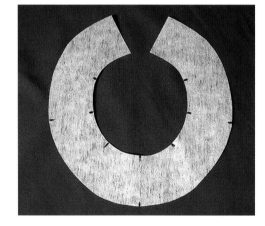

Photo 4. Brim pattern of Trilby, showing the extra notches on the collar edge of brim.

line. Start from the collar edge, to one side of the seam line, using a normal machine stitch length, and stitch all the way, up to the top and down to the collar edge on the other side. Then lift the machine foot, turn the piece crown, and stitch along the other side of the seam line in the same way. Diagram 4 shows the start of the edge stitching. Repeat the same process for the center front to back seam.

The Brim

1. Create the brim in the same manner as for the brim in Basic Hat; see sections on stitching and attaching a brim there.
2. The brim for the Trilby has extra notches at the collar edge (Photo 4). To sew on the brim, align the center front and center back seams with the notches on the brim; then align the side seam of the crown with the center side notches of the brim. Align the other notches and ease the piece crown to fit the brim. Stitch the piece crown to the brim.

Line in the same manner as for the Basic Hat.

Trilby

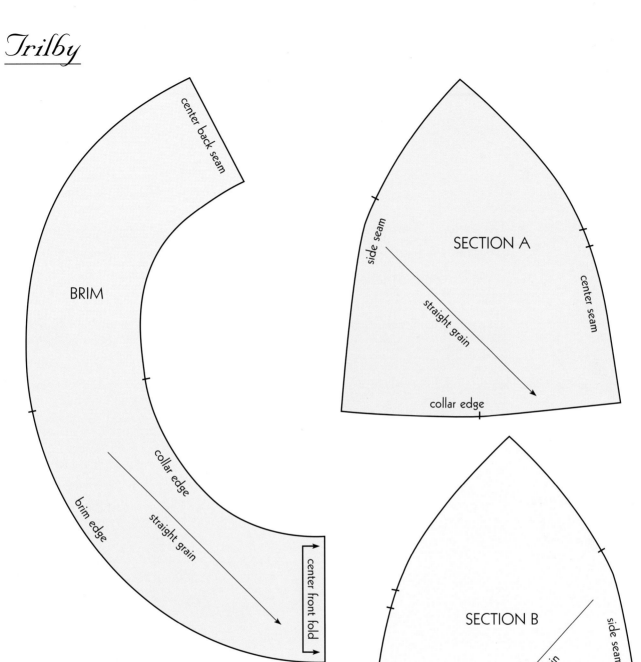

center back seam

BRIM

collar edge

brim edge

straight grain

center front fold

SECTION A

side seam

center seam

straight grain

collar edge

SECTION B

center seam

side seam

straight grain

collar edge

Patterns for the Trilby. Add seam allowances before cutting.

Country Cap

The method of making the Country Cap is the same as for the Basic Hat, so follow the instructions for the Basic Hat, with or without piping. For the peak, see the instructions in the basic Peak chapter.

Group of hats made with the Country Cap pattern. Center back, gray and black check. right front, red silk. Front, red and green check. Left, dark green silk.

Materials

✂ Fashion fabric

✂ Fusible nonwoven iron-on inter-facing

✂ Batting (wadding)

✂ Lightweight lining fabric such as taffeta

✂ Fine cord for piping*

✂ Fabric for piping*

✂ Materials for pattern making (see Pattern chapter)

Piping is optional.

Pieces to Cut

Fashion fabric + interfacing: 1 top
cap, 1 under cap, 2 peaks (1R)

Lining: 1 top cap and 1 under cap

Batting (wadding): 1 peak; split the
batting to the correct thickness

Sewing the Top Cap to the Under Cap

All construction is done with right
sides of fabric facing, unless otherwise noted.

1. Using a normal machine stitch,
   sew the center front seam of the
   under cap of fashion fabric +
   interfacing. Sew the dart in the
   top cap of fabric + interfacing
   (Diagram 1). Trim back the interfacing on both to the seam line
   that was sewn (Diagram 2).

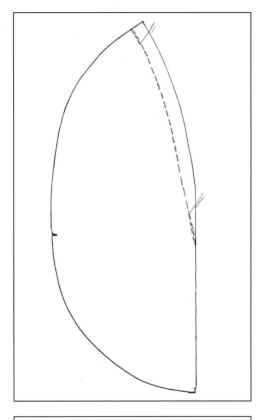

*Diagram 1. The dart in
the top cap, stitched.*

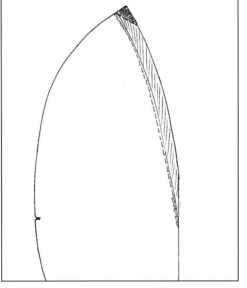

*Diagram 2. Trim the
fusible interfacing back
to the seam line on the
stitched seam, and clip
off the corner of the
seam allowance.*

Photo 1. Left, piping on top edge of under cap. Center, fusible interfacing of seam allowance trimmed to stitching line Right, top cap stitched to under cap.

2. Trim off the ends of the seam allowances at an angle and finger press the seams open. Photo 1 shows the above steps completed, with piping to the top edge of the under cap.
3. Sew the lining pieces together in the same way you did for the fabric in step 1.

Piping

Piping is optional. Make piping as described in Piping chapter. To attach piping, stitch piping as described in the Piping chapter, starting at the center back fold at the top edge of the under cap. Change the color of the bobbin thread to some other color than what is used in sewing the hat, to highlight the stitch line.

Stitching Top Cap to Under Cap

1. Pin the top cap to the under cap. **Note:** The outer edge of the top cap is slightly bigger than the under cap. This enables the top cap to roll slightly over the edge. With some fabrics it is advisable to stitch a row of ease stitching (long machine stitches) around the top cap, just inside the seam allowance. Pull one of the threads to gather the top cap slightly, so it will fit. In a normal machine stitch length, stitching on the under cap side, sew the under cap to top cap, starting at the center back fold. Slightly stretch the under cap to fit the top cap. Trim back the interfacing of the seam allowances to the stitching lines to reduce bulk.
2. Turn the cap right-side out. Steam the inside of the cap and finger-press the seams in place.

Peak

Sew the peak together as described in the basic Peak chapter. Topstitch the peak if you want to. At the center front seam, join the collar edge of the peak to the collar edge of the fashion fabric + interfacing under cap, carefully aligning notches and seam lines. Turn the cap inside out, and stitch together from the peak side.

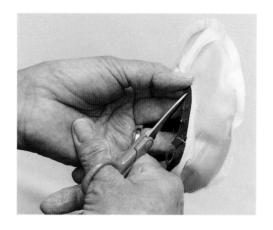

Photo 2. Clip the collar edge of the peak only.

Attaching the Lining

1. Place the cap lining and fashion fabric pieces together, right sides facing, being sure to tuck the peak in between the two.
2. On the collar edge, starting at the center back, stitch the two together.
3. Where the peak is stitched to the collar edge of the under cap, carefully clip, on an angle, on the collar edge of the peak only, every ⅜ inch (1 cm) to just within the stitching line (⅛ inch or 2 mm away); see Photo 2. This helps the peak fit around the head.
4. On the lining side, unpick the seam stitching approximately ¾ inch (2 cm) on either side of the center front seam (Diagram 3).

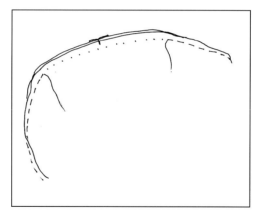

Diagram 3. Unpick a small section of the lining seam.

Photo 3. Pull the fabric cap through opening in the lining.

Photo 4. Push the lining into the inside of the cap.

Diagram 4. Slipstitch the lining seam closed.

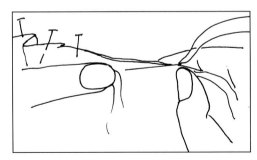

5. Pull the cap through the seam opening (Photo 3) so it is right-side out and push the lining in the cap (Photo 4). With a hand sewing needle, slipstitch the seam opening closed (Diagram 4).

6. Steam and finger-press the cap into shape.

7. On the lining side of the collar edge of the under cap, starting at one side of the peak edge, stitch a line 1/32 inch (1 mm) in from the edge, around the back, to the other peak edge (see Diagram 5 and Photo 5 and 5a). This helps to keep the collar edge flat.

8. Pull the thread tails through to the inside and stitch them in, in the same method as for brim thread ends (see Basic Hat chapter section on brims).

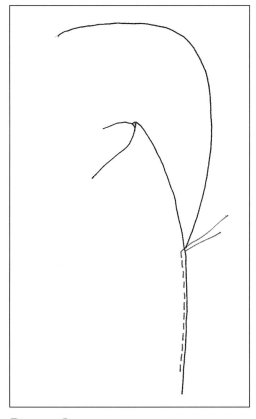

Diagram 5

Photo 5

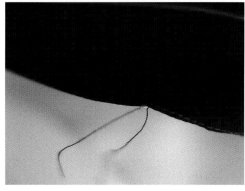

Photo 5a

Diagram 5. Stitch the edge of the cap starting from one peak edge and working around to the other.

Photo 5. The side of the cap, showing topstitching at the edge.

Photo 5a. Closeup of cap at peak edge showing topstitching near edge of cap.

Country Cap

Patterns for the Country Cap. Add seam allowances before cutting.

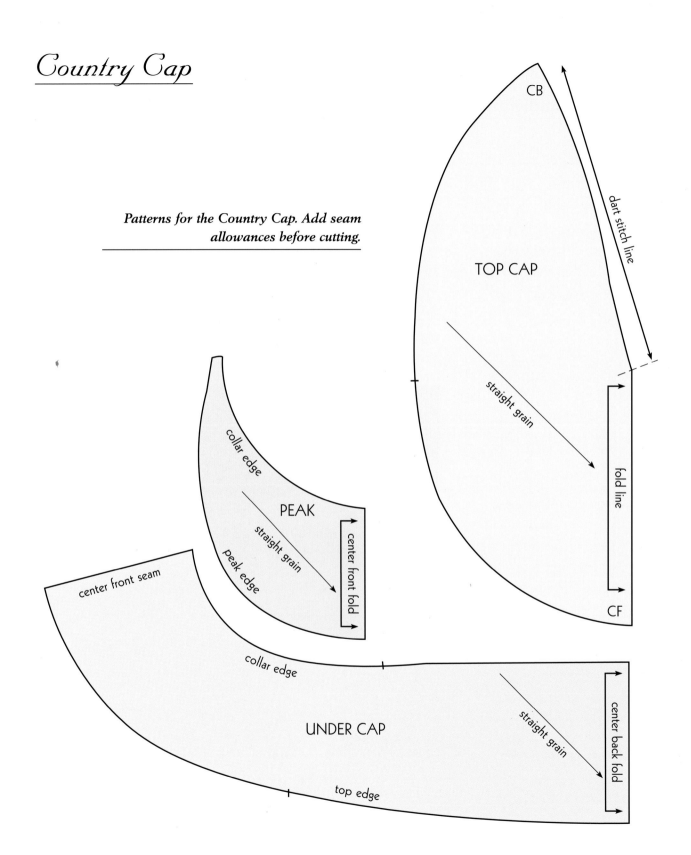

Hat Stand

Make the Hat Stand using the pattern to become familiar with the principle of the stand. Then you can enlarge it or make it whatever size you want to suit the size of the hat design. The pattern is 2 inches (5 cm) × 7 inches (18 cm). Paint the stand the color of your choice.

Materials

✄ Craft knife

✄ Ruler

✄ Strong cardboard

✄ Paint

1. Choose a strong cardboard that doesn't bend easily. Trace out the pattern and copy it to cardboard, or measure it and redraw it on the cardboard. Cut 2 pieces from cardboard, using a craft knife and a ruler.

2. Measure and mark a slot in each piece along the slot line and cut out the slot in each piece. The width of the slot should be the width of the cardboard's thickness.

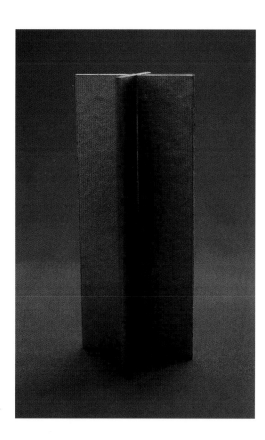

Finished hat stand

3. Put the pieces together with one like a right-side up U and one like an inverted U to create the stand (photos 1 and 2) to be sure they fit.

4. Take the pieces apart and paint as desired; then reassemble.

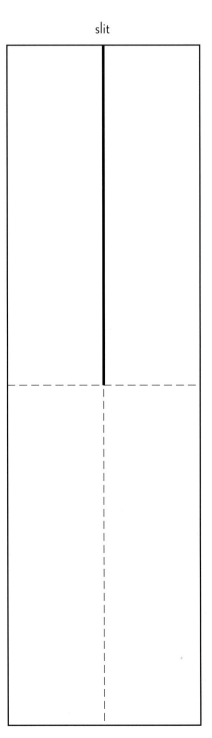

slit

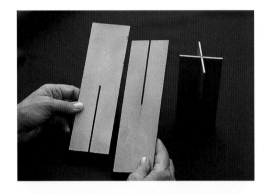

Photo 1. The two parts of the stand.

Photo 2. The two parts fitted together.

Pattern for the Hat Stand. Cut 2 from cardboard.

Useful Tables

METRIC TABLE

Inches	mm	cm	Inches	mm	cm
⅛	3	0.3	5	127	12.7
¼	6	0.6	6	152	15.2
⅜	10	1.0	7	178	17.8
½	13	1.3	8	203	20.3
⅝	16	1.6	9	229	22.9
¾	19	1.9	10	254	25.4
⅞	22	2.2	11	279	27.9
1	25	2.5	12	305	30.5
1¼	32	3.2	13	330	33.0
1½	38	3.8	14	356	35.6
1¾	44	4.4	15	381	38.1
2	51	5.1	16	406	40.6
2½	64	6.4	17	432	43.2
3	76	7.6	18	457	45.7
3½	89	8.9	19	483	48.3
4	102	10.2	20	508	50.8
4½	114	11.4			

YARDS INTO INCHES

Yards	Inches	Yards	Inches
⅛	4.5	1⅛	40.5
¼	9	1¼	45
⅜	13.5	1⅜	49.5
½	18	1½	54
⅝	22.5	1⅝	58.5
¾	27	1¾	63
⅞	31.5	1⅞	67.5
1	36	2	72

Index